THE RETURN OF CABBAGE ALLEY: STORIES OF JUNE VICTORY

AS TOLD TO THOMAS BRENT ANDREWS

CHRONIC DISCONTENT BOOKS
FRANKLIN, TENNESSEE

THE RETURN OF CABBAGE ALLEY

Published January 2020 by Chronic Discontent Books
Franklin, Tennessee

ISBN 978-0-9767056-6-6

Library of Congress Control Number 2020901402

Cover design and production by Jeff Hottle

Contents designed by Ginny Andrews

With photos from the Vera Sterling collection; by Amy Geszvain; and by Brent Andrews. The cover photo is from the Vera Sterling collection, and shows the Bayou Band at Cabbage Alley, Uptown New Orleans, circa 1973. Pictured are June Victory on guitar, Norwood "Geechie" Johnson on percussion, and Preston "Dog" Adams on the drum kit (back cover).

The Chronic Discontent Books logo is borrowed from *Ancient Sichuan and the Unification of China*, by Steven F. Sage, State University of New York Press, 1992. The bone inscription is believed to be approximately 3,200 years old. Writes Sage: "Conjecture relates this eye to a legendary version of Shu origins, mentioning a 'vertical-eyed man' (*zong mu zhi ren*), figuratively perhaps meaning a 'man of vision.' "

We dedicate this book to our dads—the late Wilson "Vic" Victorian, Sr., and William Franklin Andrews—who taught us about life and nourished our talents.

Uncle Willy's Guitar

Down on the bayou, flag is on fire.
Cochise coming, soldiers all running.
Me and my Spyboy, sitting on the side.
Watching trouble, passing us by.

- June Victory and the Bayou Renegades, 'Down On the Bayou'

Wilson Victorian, Jr.—June Victory—is a guitar player and songwriter from New Orleans. He is an outlaw, a Mardi Gras Indian, and a hero. He is a brother and a son, a father and a good friend. His face is bronze, spotted with tiny freckles, without too many wrinkles, considering the miles on the man. Today he is clean-shaven, but he often wears a mustache. His mid-length hair hangs in braids, under a black Oakley trucker hat. He is dressed in a white button-down shirt, left unbuttoned over a black T-shirt, and white pants over tennis shoes. He has cut a dime-sized piece out of the back of his cheek, shaving this morning, but he is no longer bleeding, and is still confident enough to wear white. Our conversation begins under the blue sky on a patio off Tchoupitoulas Street two blocks from Tipitina's, where June has played many times.

"I was born Sept. 29th, 1949. My mother and father,

Wilson and Mildred Victorian, were raised up in a place called False River, the island up in New Roads, Louisiana, about thirty-five miles outside of Baton Rouge," June says. "It was mostly French Creole. And they moved to New Orleans when they were real young, and had a baby girl. That was my sister, Vera, and she was born on Valentine's Day. Later on, here I come: June Victory.

"As far back as I can remember, I believed when God gives people a gift, it's real," he says.

"I remember living on Third Street, off of Claiborne and Jackson. I didn't know nothing about guitars. Then we were living on Philip Street and Willow, and they had a guy named William who used to sell vegetables. 'I got lettuce and tomatoes, ladies' " (in a singsong voice). "And they used to have these crates. I'd bust the crates up and take the sticks and put rubber bands on them and just play with it, plucking and plucking. I was about six years old.

"And after a while we moved to Washington and South Dorgenois, to a place called the Plaza Towers. I had to have been about seven. From there, we went on South Derbigny Street, off of Claiborne, across from Taylor Park. It was a private park, for whites only. It was a mixed neighborhood, but a little better. Because my mom looked white, and my dad was black: We had to fight both sides, blacks and whites. And they had a lot of bullies, and when my mom and dad would go to work in the summertime, we'd be home alone, me and my sister, and the kids would come around there, trying to hound-up, acting crazy and stuff.

"My sister was going to a Catholic school on First and Galvez. (St. Monica's.) Pretty soon I got in—

kindergarten. And it was like around a public school for the Calliope housing project, so we had a hard time with that, because a lot of fighting was going on at that school. It was rough in that neighborhood. Me myself, I remember going to school—didn't learn nothing. My mind was on something else, I guess.

"My mom never wanted us to socialize with kids, and as a matter of fact, my sister was crazy about Indians, and she didn't allow her to entertain or get involved with Mardi Gras Indians, nothing like this. But Vera would always sneak off and try to follow them around, on Mardi Gras Day. And then we had family members that masked Indian, like first cousins: the Black Eagles, my cousins Curly and Geneva.

"One day my aunt gave me a little plastic flute thing, and I would play, and my sister started hearing things. It sounded pretty good. And my mom took me to my uncle's house, and he had a guitar. He was an older man. He was learning how to play.

"His name was Uncle Willy, and he was married to Geneva, and he had a little daughter named Cynthia. So anyway my mom and the family used to take turns going by different family members' houses on the weekends, and they would party and drink and the kids would be in a certain spot. I never hung with the kids.

"But I walked in there and I seen this guitar in the bed. So they was in the back, and you know how a kid tampers with things. I was eight years old. And I picked it up, and I went in the front, sat on the floor, and I didn't know what I was doing. But the next thing I knew, my mom, dad, aunt, uncle were running into the front room. When I picked my head up, the family members was surrounded around me, and my Aunt Geneva was sitting on the floor with her legs crossed, looking. And when I raised up my head and I seen her, she looked at me, she screamed and she flipped over! And everybody said, 'Wow, oh, wow, oh wow!' So I'm figuring out what's going on! They say I was playing!

"It so happened, the next morning when I woke up to go to school, the guitar was in my bed. Uncle Willy gave the guitar to my dad, and he gave it to me. I'll never forget Uncle Willy for that.

"My first guitar—it was an acoustic guitar. And he went and bought him an electric one.

"So I'm playing, at eight years old, and I'm studying, fooling with it. Catching on. I can play the guitar.

"So I'm sitting in the alley—don't want to play with the kids, go in the park. Just fooling with this guitar, day after day.

"And my sister had an old juke-box 45, and she would put the records on and I would play. It didn't take me no time to learn. Plus sing it!

"I was taking the guitar with me to school every day, learning nothing, just jamming. And I wanted to sing so what I did, I took a receiver off a landline, cut it, put the jack on it and plugged it into an amp; and there it was: I had a microphone.

"Boy, my momma liked to had a fit when she came home! And my dad, that was a big joke to him!

"I'd never been to (music) school, so my parents said we need to put him in some kind of school or something, see what he can do. And they sent me to Houston music school. To a man named Walter Epps. I didn't learn how to read at that time. But I had a certain style.

"He tried to teach me to bend my fingers a certain

way to do a bar chord, but I just couldn't do it. I had a certain way of bending my fingers on majors and minors, double-octave style, playing rhythm. So he said, 'Just follow me.' And he would start playing, and there I go.

"He spent a lot of time with me. And it got so I was doing pretty good in school, and at home, and my dad went to Epps and said, 'You think he's ready for an electric guitar?' And Epps said, 'Sure.' And my dad bought me my first electric guitar. It was a Dean Electron, with lipstick pickup.

"It got to where my people couldn't afford the lesson anymore and Epps said, 'Don't worry about the money. I tell you what I'm gonna do. I want him to come to my house every Saturday, about ten in the morning, and I'll work him over.' And he did. And what he would do, he would sit me in his house and show me all kind of pictures in this big photo album, of when he was working with famous people, big concerts, a lifestyle of him playing with big bands and he would just show me these pictures of him when he was young. He was playing around the country with all kinds of bands: big bands, Count Basie, you name them. Big stars, and he was the guitar player. I said, 'Wow, this is what I want to do.' And he kept going through them and I kept looking at these pictures and then we would sit down and play a few things.

"And he would ask me, 'Do this, do that,' and I couldn't. But he said, 'Go and do what you wanna do, and I'll follow you.' He started letting me do what I wanted to do with the guitar and he started following me and something caught on.

"He took me to a show where the music teachers would pick one of the students out of all these music schools to perform with. And we won first place. At ten, eleven years old I was making money, playing music with my teacher.

"I'll never forget this man: Walter Epps. He was a music teacher, and I loved him for the chance that he gave me to develop my own style. And I do have my own style. He let me lead.

"He let me lead, as a child. And at fourteen years old I ran away from home and went to making money to support my mom and my dad. I've been gone ever since."

Vee Fire Queen

Vera Sterling is a widely respected Mardi Gras Indian Big Queen of the Creole Wild West tribe, welcomed and loved by many Indian tribes. Each year and with great effort she dons a new and elaborate suit to mask as Vee Fire Queen for Mardi Gras Day and Super Sunday. On this Mardi Gras Day she is freezing cold and fussy. She is seventy-three, a wise and vocal elder, tall and thin and with no patience for nonsense. She is free to complain and does so liberally. She grouses that the Big Chief made a fan for another Queen, but did not make one for her, and seems ready to carve him a new one over it. She looks resplendent, beyond beautiful, yes, royal in her feathers and patches, silk and fur—and she is checking every stitch.

She sits a while to warm up in a car by Sadie's Beauty Salon on Jackson Avenue, midmorning on a very brisk, but sunny, Mardi Gras Day. The Zulu parade has already passed. She caught two coconuts. Now dressed in her suit, she keeps searching it for signs of glue-gun work, and if she finds any the Big Chief's ears will be burning. She looks up to the street and is astonished, then furious, to see a gorgeous Big Queen walk by with pockets on her suit that Big Chief "Little Walter" Cook made with love and care, which Vee Fire Queen feels he neglected to put into her own suit. "I bet those pockets aren't just flaps of fabric, either," she tells her adult daughter, Schelita White—today, a lady-in-waiting to her mother, lovingly assisting in this unique tradition. "I bet he lined those pockets!"

Vee Fire Queen expects only great work from Chief Little Walter. His beading, dying and sewing is in high demand in the Indian community. Vera describes Walter as "head of the class" when it comes to making Indian suits. His dyes are of particularly good quality. "Two-tone, three-tone, any color you want, he can do it. I've seen it with my own eyes," she later tells me.

Vee Fire Queen holds a place of influence among New Orleans Indians. One time June and I were trying to get across town on Mardi Gras Day before the Zulu parade, and running late. The main streets being subject to blockage by floats and construction, traffic and police, we took the backstreets, June giving the directions and me behind the wheel. After a few turns we got caught on a street with a big Mardi Gras Indian gathering going on, the Indians in the street in front of the recently rebuilt Magnolia Projects, now Harmony Oaks. There were masked Indians, drummers and such, in full stride, and a lot of people gathered. At June's direction I pulled up close—but the Indians do not part easily, when they are out like this. Fire trucks and police cars can get through, but nothing less official.

June jumped out of the car and went over and spoke with the people on this side of the group. For a moment they did not look inclined to cooperate, then some began to fall back and gesture and by the time June got back to the car they had cleared a path for us to get through.

"How did you get them to do that?" I asked as we drove through the provided space between the marchers, musicians and Indians arrayed in brilliant suits.

"I mentioned my sister," said June.

For Vee Fire Queen Mardi Gras Day means rushing to Sadie's Beauty Salon early in the morning, in time to watch Zulu and see the Zulu King; then spending a long time getting dressed in her Indian suit, then spending a long time more waiting for the Big Chief, always wary of rain that could ruin her day and her suit and often wondering aloud what is keeping the Big Chief.

Today each Queen compliments the other on her beautiful suit as they meet by Ms. Sadie's before moving with the Big Chief. They stop to pose for pictures with many admirers. In a life of bad days and good days, this is one of the good ones.

Chief Little Walter emerges from his mother's salon, grand and grandiose in peach silk and turquoise beads and ostrich-feather crown, long side-braids falling toward his waistline. He is accompanied by men carrying pieces of his suit. There are *oohs* and *ahhs* of wonder from the relieved crowd standing around waiting for this moment. There are many pictures to pose for now, with friends and strangers, with people who have helped all year and tourists the Indians have never met. Chief Little Walter and his people pose patiently and smile.

Once things get moving on the street, following the Big Chief, Vee Fire Queen walks with her head held high and a serious look on her face. She is prepared from the tallest feather to her silk- and bead-dressed boots. This year she is in peach silk, with peach fur trim, a broad apron depicting a Native American (he is either dancing with a blond-haired fellow, or about to strike him down), a jewelled necklace and matching headband, and high orange feathers behind. Silk extends down both arms, which also carry banners of fur-lined fabric. An additional, intricately beaded set of arms reaches down her front. All over are turquoise accents. There is a white dove, wings outstretched, on each of her shoulders. She takes advantage of her naturally flashy hair, leaving it uncovered. It is a rich burgundy color, with tight, short curls.

The Big Chiefs empower their people with their manly displays. They go out ready to face-off with another Big Chief if they meet on the street. They will shout, sing, and brag about their suits and their Queens. They vie to be the "prettiest." In a city where suffering has touched everyone, the people will remember how powerful their Big Chief was all year long and look forward to seeing him again Mardi Gras Day, and it will help see them through the year. They will remember how instead of engaging in physical combat with the opposing Big Chief, the less powerful Big Chief nodded his respect and did the hardest thing a man can do, suit or no suit: stand down with honor and dignity, so as not to ruin the day for the people.

The preening competitions of the Big Chiefs replaced the knife-and-hatchet work of the past, when Mardi Gras Indian battles were not so figurative and verbal, colorful and even marketable, but were sometimes bloody brawls. The change was the work of visionary Big Chiefs such as Allison "Tootie" Montana, who stressed beadwork and flamboyance, over violence. In time that approach brought the support and cooperation of city leaders. These stories are told elsewhere. The efforts might have spared New Orleans a conclusive battle between the forces of law and order and the preservation of history and culture.

The Big Chiefs might seem like braggarts on Mardi

Gras Day—shouting and taking over the streets. But in return they are humble servants to the community the rest of the year. A Big Chief might attend a wake in his suit to honor a community member who has passed, adding music and color and pageantry to the memorial party. Children will stand in wonder and awe at his suit and his song and his drummers and his Big Queen, forgetting their grief for a while. He might bring food to the needy. He might help someone with legal paperwork, if he has talent in that area. He will visit the sick, make a phone call for you, and suffer with you.

It is not unusual for a Big Chief to have more than one Big Queen behind him. The Big Queens are free to walk behind the Big Chief they admire and respect. They are selective, and judgmental. They keep an eye out for Big Chiefs who do not seem to have the peoples' interests in mind. And once behind a chief, they are his most fervent supporters and staunchest protectors. Without the Big Queens the Big Chief could find himself alone on the streets: The one who does not keep this in mind risks a lot.

As Vee Fire Queen walks along Jackson Avenue, behind the Big Chief, but preceding the Indian rhythm section of bass drum and tambourines, she soaks up compliments from every quarter: "Beautiful suit, honey." "Girl, that is so pretty."

And she dances. She steps this way and that, forward and backward. She marches in place, grooving with her arms and legs and whole body to the beat of the drums. Colors flash, feathers ripple as she dances. She might dance behind the Big Chief for hours, as he visits certain watering holes and elders' homes, and faces other Big Chiefs in the streets; or she might bolt at the whiff of foul weather or trouble. Vee Fire Queen reserves all the prerogatives due a Queen, and leaving is one of them.

I walk with the Indians along Jackson Avenue and into the residential blocks of the surrounding neighborhood, as part of the group of family and friends, and a few tourists following the colorful parade. The big crowd here for Zulu is gone; there are few people out on the sidewalks and sometimes nobody at all. When we are in the sun, it is warm and welcome. The shade feels like a bath of cold water. People open their doors to see the Indians pass, then go back inside. Most of the people at this parade are involved. There are many colorful Indians but I don't see a Spyboy. He could be ranging ahead, on the lookout for other gangs, and I was too late to catch even his shadow. There was once a Shadow Boy, who backed up the Big Chief, but it is rare to see one now. The Creole Wild West, said to be the oldest Mardi Gras Indian tribe, has been parading for more than a third of the city's three-hundred-year history. The Creole Wild West is not as numerous as it used to be as Indian culture has expanded to so many tribes nobody can keep count. Chiefs branch out and start their own tribes, sometimes called gangs. June estimates there are thirty thousand New Orleans Indians. His is an Uptown, beaded-Indian culture; there is also the Downtown, 3-D culture. While the description does not apply in every case, generally Uptown, beaded tribes adopt North American animals such as the grey wolf and golden eagle for their emblems. Downtown, 3-D tribes include African and Asian animals such as lions and tigers in their imagery. Their differences are both dramatic and visible and quiet and tucked away in wounded pride or broken hearts. But they would be more powerful together than they can ever be isolated and apart, as June sees it.

This Mardi Gras Day we have a Big Chief, Second Chiefs including June, some powerful enough to be Big Chiefs in their own right, and our proud Queens. We have a Wild Man in horned headdress, as fierce as anybody's Wild Man. From beside his black skull mask drop two golden braids, tempering his ferocious look. His broad, tall, yellow-and-orange colors suggest a ball of fire. The tribe is safe, with a Wild Man like this at the ready. I am afraid for him to catch me taking a picture with my phone, so I wait until he is distracted saying hello to June, and take my chance. I rush away and don't notice, but later, looking back at the picture, the Wild Man is pointing at me, and I wonder about his message.

We have child Queens dressed as elaborately as their elders. Sometimes the little Queens struggle to carry their suits and get help from a brother or sister. The little Queen looks perfectly at home in her suit of silk and feathers: Her helper looks a bit uncomfortable, dressed normally but carrying a big feathered crown.

And we have pounding, dramatic music. Dressed in a black suit jacket with sequins, and a cowboy hat in purple, green and gold, the Mardi Gras colors, June sings into a toy megaphone beside the Indian drummers. Sometimes I sit in with my Sunday school tambourine, from Shuff's Music in Franklin, Tennessee. Mostly I walk alongside and watch. I am dressed in my French Quarter outfit, a white Oxford shirt and black pants, which I wear to blend in with the waiters down there dressed the same. It is a workingman's suit. Today I have added a silk tie with peach stripes to match Vee Fire Queen.

June's toy megaphone has a siren feature: He whirs the siren a lot as we walk and it fits perfectly within the pounding of the drums. He plays the siren like an instrument, finding spaces between drum beats to let it wail. He clowns and looks around.

Everyone joins in singing:

"Creole Wild West, Creole Wild West!
Creole Wild West, Creole Wild West!"

The song comes very smoothly to the ear, eliminating most of the sharp consonants. It sounds like:

"Creole Wil' Weeees, Creole Wil' Wess'!
Creole Wil' Weeees, Creole Wil' Wess'!"

There is drumming and dancing, and everywhere I look, smiling, happy faces.

June sings "Shoo Fly," a traditional folk song lyrically transformed into an Angola Prison song, accompanied by drums and tambourines and a cowbell. June sings the lead, and everyone joins full-throated for the recurring chorus:

"Early that morning 'bout a quarter to nine"
"Shoo fly, don't bother me!"
"The dirty old judge gave me some time!"
"Shoo fly, don't bother me!"
"Early that morning, nobody did know"
"Shoo fly, don't bother me!"
"I shot my pistol through the jailhouse door."
"Shoo fly, don't bother me!"
"They took me down to a valley so low"

"Shoo fly, don't bother me!"
"We were hitting that cane, row-by-row."
"Shoo fly, don't bother me!"
"I met a chicken-boy called One Eyed Jack"
"Shoo fly, don't bother me!"
"If he hits you, you gotta hit him back."
"Shoo fly, don't bother me!"
"His boyfriend named Big Head Joe"
"Shoo fly, don't bother me!"
"Don't take no chance, use a two-by-fo'."

The drums pound, Vee Fire Queen dances, a real police siren consumes the air. Everyone looks around, including Chief Little Walter who, seeing no threat, throws June a delighted smile that shows the weight of the work is now off Walter's talented shoulders, and the Indians are running.

Chief Little Walter, June, followers—everybody sings: "Shoo fly, don't bother me!"

Junior

Sixty-five years ago, way uptown in New Orleans and long before she became Vee Fire Queen, Vera shared a twin bed every night with her little brother, nicknamed "June" for "junior" and four years younger, in a house on South Derbigny Street across from Taylor Park. She doesn't remember if it was a whites-only park. If so, few people paid attention to that. She did remember that June liked to suck his thumb and did not want to give it up. Vera tried putting hot sauce on the thumb, to get him to stop. It did not work.

Vera protected June from dangers real and imagined. He nestled beside her to sleep at night, sucking his thumb and pulling gently on her earlobe. He had a habit of pulling on her ear, something she tolerated since it kept him quiet. He knew better than to pull hard. She liked to wear earrings and one morning awoke and they were out. She looked around, "Where are my earrings?" She found them in the bed. June had taken them out in the night. He did that more than once, Vera recalls.

One time while she was going to school at St. Monica's, which she attended through eighth grade, two New Orleans Police Department officers brought June to the school looking for Vera, and then brought him home since school had already let out. They had found June wandering the city.

"He was just a little kid at the time," she says. "When they brought him home, they said, 'He was singing on the way over in the police cruiser.' So I said, 'What was he singing?'

"The police said to June, 'Tell her what you were singing.'

"And he started singing, 'You ain't nothing but a hound dog.' "

Vera caught on to June's talent before the others. She remembers when he was about nine years old, around 1958, and she used to use her weekly allowance—"all of it"—to buy the latest 45 rpm records, many of which she still has today. She would bring June into her room to listen to the new James Brown, Chubby Checker, or B.B. King release and he would soon have the guitar part figured out and be playing it there in her bedroom.

She remembers the first time he was able to pluck one of those songs out with his little fingers as she stood there, incredulous. "I ran over to him and gave him a big kiss on his cheek, and I said, 'We're going to be rich, June!' "

Vera remembers her brother playing so well "behind the records." She wrote down the words and he would sing, too. She encouraged her parents to send June to school "so he could read music."

She told her parents, "June is playing the blues."

She recalled her dad keeping an account at the corner grocery run by the Fortunatos. She and June could go there any time and get what they wanted. They had more than some of the others in the neighborhood, so they shared with less fortunate friends. Their favorite thing to get at the Fortunato store was French bread with hot dogs, covered in chili. Vera and June wore custom-made clothes when they were teenagers, purchased from one of the tailors on Canal Street. She says her parents bought her a car when she was fifteen, and they bought one for June when he was seventeen.

Her brother's first fan, Vera followed June as he became a nightclub star and still follows him now that he is a senior citizen. She has followed him to clubs all over town and beyond, on the most special occasions wearing her Vee Fire Queen regalia, and always delighting people with her dance moves.

She remembers burning June's music onto CDs and selling them for five dollars at his shows, "making good little change." She has organized a busload of people from New Orleans to attend a False River show featuring Ernie K-Doe and June, and says everybody made money. She offers a partial list of places around New Orleans where June has played: House of Blues, G.T.O., Club 77, La Parisian Room, Praline Connection, 809 Club, Ernie K-Doe's club, Irma Thomas' club on Gravier Street, the Fox bar, "Ira's house" and recently, a new Uptown club called Portside Lounge, and Bamboula's on Frenchmen Street.

Vera, the proud sister, remembers when June started playing shows those many years ago. She carried his guitar to every one. People used to think she was in the band, and she never had to pay.

Playing Grand Isle

June is telling about the first time he left home.

"What happened, I met a guy, they called him Jimmy, he was a drummer. He was with some gangsters up in Grand Isle. The guy's name was Tony. He owned a club there on the beach where people would come and swim on the beach at Grand Isle. And he used to have boats coming in from all over.

"He used to hire people like James Brown, Jackie Wilson, Bobby 'Blue' Band. One night I went there and he had a double band, Ernie K-Doe, all kinds of famous people. I was the opening act. I didn't have a band.

"So he had a lot of tents out there. And the musicians and the groups would sleep in the tents, right on the beach, and he would feed you like big old hamburgers and give you a cold drink—that's all you would have to eat.

"He said, 'I'm going to let you play with all the major groups that come in here, and sit in,' and he brought Joe Tex, one of the baddest musicians they got. He was cold. He was from Texas. He was better than James Brown. All these guys learned from Joe Tex how to work the stage, and dance around.

"I was sitting in with Joe Tex, James Brown, Jackie Wilson, and I was making a hundred dollars a day. My people caught up with me and they brought me back home because I was young. And they put me on a bus with a lot of other teenagers and they sent us away to a camp in Texas to try to get us straight. And I was the youngest one. We were sitting up there eating breakfast one day, and girls used to come in there. A girl came in, I was talking to some guys and laughing, she must have thought I was talking about her. The next thing I know she came charging up to me with a butcher knife. She said, 'I heard what you said!' She was running at me—I was eating grits and drinking some coffee—and I jumped up and hit her with some hot coffee and grits. And that slowed her down!

"The people said, 'You've gotta quit fooling with this girl!'

"I said, 'I didn't do her nothing!'

"They knew I couldn't swim. They threw all my clothes and suitcase in the pool, soaking wet. And they put me in lockdown.

"A guy named Larry Schmidt and some other guys jumped me. I was fighting these three guys, jumping on the bed, fighting, swinging, and an old man came in. His name was Chief. And they all stopped fighting, and one of them tried to run, and I put my foot out and kicked one of them and his head went straight through the sheetrock. He was looking like he was dead! He pulled his head out of the hole and said, 'Aw, sh-,' and everybody started laughing!

"So I went back to Tony, I had a job again, and I stayed away for about six months. We had no way to spend money out there: a thousand miles from anywhere. So Tony said, 'I'm going to give you fifty a shift—anytime you walk in, grab a guitar, that's fifty dollars.' So I went in and played a show. Then I sat in for another show—that's a hundred. Then another man played, and I sat in, and sat in again, I made about two hundred and fifty dollars that day. So the money started piling up.

"I had a briefcase full of money. I came back to my mom's house. And I had a drawer full of money. And I was about fifteen. My mom would come to me and say, 'June, is it all right if I borrow a hundred dollars, can I borrow this and can I borrow that?' We were living in a shack on South Derbigny Street. I said, 'Mom, take what you want.'

"But I wasn't working. I was getting out of hand. I started to get into drugs. I was going to a place at Washington and Magnolia, and there were a lot of drugs running around there. And my dad would come and drag my car home, cussing at me. Dad said, 'How much money you making?'

"He said, 'Why don't you get into your own business, so you don't have to work for anybody anymore?'

"I said, 'That takes money!' "

"He said, 'You've got money!' "

"I said, 'I need a truck, and tools,' and I got all kinds of tools for lawn mowing. But I still wasn't working.

"So my friends were showing me where they'd bought houses and all this. I went to my dad and gave him five thousand dollars, and my mother borrowed another five thousand from the owner of the grocery store where she was head cashier, at Washington and Claiborne. She found a house on the Parkway, and the lady sold it to her for twenty five thousand dollars. That's forty years ago. My daddy kept some of the money. He bought a Lincoln, and a nice car for my mom, which was smart: He wanted to get into the middle class."

His dad came in one day and said June had a choice:

" 'Go back to school, or go find a job, or come work for me.' If not one of those, 'Pack your clothes and get out of my house.'

"And I said, 'Man, I done put him on this street!'

"But I appreciate what he done. No matter what your children do for you, you're still a parent. That doesn't mean you're going to let him do whatever he wants to do, and lose your self-respect. My mom heard that and she was so sad, and I didn't want to get my mom and dad into it, so I left."

Kin-Folks, Dog, and Lobo Guitar

Reservation people, time to move away.
Heard through the grapevine, that we can't stay.
If you see my Spyboy, tell him stay out of town.
I'll catch up with him, 'fore the sun go down.
Down on the bayou, where we all come from.

-June Victory and the Bayou Renegades, 'Down On the Bayou'

June is talking and singing in the car on the way back to New Orleans from the Baton Rouge area. He has been visiting his people and playing at a nightclub outside New Roads called Kin-Folks.

After leaving New Roads via the marvelous John James Audubon Bridge over the Mississippi River and negotiating the traffic of Baton Rouge we're traveling I-10 eastbound through thick woods and swampy scenes and I drive very carefully. There could be anything out here in the swamps: monsters, anything. June talks of a snapping turtle bigger than a house they found out here. The government carried it away on a flatbed railroad car.

June's voice sounds scratchy and terrible. He's been up at least twenty-four hours, capped off by the last hour of playing guitar and singing at Kin-Folks, and he is telling stories.

Kin-Folks is a family nightclub, humble but hopping. On a wet and cold Sunday afternoon in spring, fronted by a gravel parking lot that was mostly puddle, the simple rectangle with extensive deferred maintenance supported a cheerful crowd, and everyone was glad to see June since he had not been there in a while.

June did not disappoint, delivering a set of electric guitar funk and Mardi Gras Indian songs that made everybody shake, or at least shake their heads. June believes in dressing flashy for shows, "to give people something to look at." Today he wore a white button hat; orange button-down shirt with black collar and bamboo pattern; a gold chain necklace; white pants and white leather shoes.

Vee Fire Queen was also on hand dancing in two colors, violet and white, long feathers abounding and another, white-dressed Queen beaded on her front. Brother picked guitar to throw sparks, sister caught his beat and turned this way and that way in the light, the violet blending with the blood-red walls of the room at different times as she danced, so that she was sometimes half-a-Queen dressed in white.

"One month my first cousin has the club, the next month another might have the club," June says on the long ride back to New Orleans. "We take turns. Everybody makes money, you know."

He played with an ad-hoc band consisting of musicians who happened to be in New Roads and up for a jam session.

"Same thing they do in New Orleans," he explains.

It sounded like they'd been playing together forever.

"It's talent," June says. "That's what it's about. You know, music is a universal thing, if you look at it. They are born with a gift. These guys can't read music. It's not nothing nobody can teach you, it's just something you born to do. It's a feeling. I read music, I write music. And with these guys, I can only write alphabet notes, they only know alphabet notes, not music notes. But it's not nothing nobody can teach you. You're just grounded like that."

I was lucky to see June reunite and play with Dog, Preston Adams, his original drummer, who had not played drums in about thirty years. Dog sat down and played a solid show.

"He built up his courage," June explains. "Now Dog, I took him to France. And he couldn't make it. The first night on the gig, he was so excited when they opened the curtains on the stage for us to kick off, the concert was over: He raised his hands and walked off the stage. It was crazy.

"And another thing I've seen about Dog: He's left-footed, right-handed. He don't like to switch up."

A drummer can be a hot item in New Orleans: June considers the city a drummer's town. The drummer can also be controversial, or get stolen, or burn out.

The Kin-Folks show was a way to get Dog back behind his kit. Promoted by John Christoff, the set featured June and Paul Resor on guitars, Earl Nunez on bass, Dog on drums, Loy Givens on saxophone, Barbara Lyon, and Leroy Toussaint.

"I just felt that he needed my support," June says. "He'd been paralyzed, he'd been hurt. And I always could come get Dog. I know he can get back in it. He can do it.

"Me myself, I wish I had support like that. I was paralyzed for six months. They prayed against me recovering. I didn't have nobody to come in and motivate me. They said I wouldn't walk again. And the only thing that got me walking was I didn't like scary movies. They wouldn't change the channel and I woke up, and I started moving. I was so spooked when I heard a noise in the house and I jumped up and ran!"

He says when his mother saw him walking again, she cried, because she knew he would return to a dangerous lifestyle.

In the back of the car is another of June's old friends. It's a black electric guitar that travels inside a coffin-shaped case much worn from adventures.

"It's a B.C. Rich, the Warlock version. They only made twenty-six in the world. I modified that one," June says. "Now the coffin case, not preaching it like it is, but we built it to put it in with my funeral the day I die. That's what I planned on. And that's going to be nice. The coffin case is going to be buried, itself.

"The guitar is for my daughter. I call her Lobo, just like you would name your dog Lobo. She's the baby. And she learned how to play guitar, and I told her she could have it. Like, 'That's Lobo guitar.' And it's in a coffin case. And that case going to be buried with me, the day I leave.

"You know, people make plans. It's a wonderful thing that you can live, and know what's gonna happen at your funeral."

Ghost Guitar

I am driving June through the neighborhood where we both live: Riverside in Uptown New Orleans. It is a dream to be driving these streets with June, and listening to his stories. With the help of June and other friends who have adopted me here I am getting to know this city like it is my own. There is a utilitarian beauty in the regular street grid that carries on mile after mile with angles to get around the river bends. Because of the river bend there are streets that disappear and reappear according to the availability of space, in keeping with the regular pattern. Some streets become other streets, and then become themselves again, as in: North Peters Street, heading upriver from the Marigny, becomes Decatur Street for a few blocks between the French Quarter and the Mississippi River, then emerges as itself again, neat as you please. You could say North Peters Street borrows Decatur Street for a few blocks.

Uptown, upriver in the Riverside neighborhood, short residential blocks go on and on lined with one- and two-story homes of many colors in many phases of repair, fronted most of the time by an inviting sidewalk. Here and there is a bargain-in-the-rough or a dilapidated shotgun house worth two hundred thousand dollars for the site: less than one-tenth of an acre that holds water all winter. It's still a bargain, compared to some cities, for a bit of land within walking distance to grocery stores and restaurants, galleries, parks, public transportation, and Mardi Gras parades.

Weeds can overtake a driveway in a month, and overgrow a house in a couple of years. Nails pop out of weathered roofs and boards and land near the street, to be moved by water and wind into the way of soft tires. Everything that loves sun and sky and humidity thrives here. There are trees weighted down with bananas and lemons and spotted with satsumas—delicious little oranges. I've seen a flock of wild parakeets eating overripe, dripping figs nobody has bothered to pick, a jealous dog standing below hoping the birds knock one loose. Trees emerge from small spaces between homes then reach out prolifically to the glorious blue sky providing shade for two neighbors and when the sun is right, both sides of the street. Roaches grow to intimidating size, wharf rats crawl along power lines, termites swarm so you have to weigh the safety and security of outdoor lighting against a flying horde making a night spot out of your porch light. The earth moves and your new pool leaks into the gutter and there are flooded streets after rain showers. In a city supporting a fathomless stream of money, these Uptown streets are so full of potholes you will hit one and bust the heck out of a tire, and be complaining about it at the tire store, when another customer looks up and says she also hit a pothole, and the replacement is going to cost fifty dollars! June and I bump along at a slow pace and that is fine with me. There is so much to see.

We are headed north on Robert Street toward Magazine, lakebound, but you can't go all the way to Magazine Street because Robert Street has been cut through and there are orange-clad workers looking at the cut. "Turn here!" June yells and I turn right on

Annunciation Street. I drive downtown-bound on Annunciation Street, crossing Soniat and Upperline and then passing the Wisner Park dog-run.

"That's where we met, June," I mention.

"It's a good thing, too, for both of us," he says. "This park used to be a slum. It was full of old, slum houses, falling down. And trouble. Drugs."

It now makes a picturesque scene, in which folks are willing to invest. Adjacent homes are bringing around half-a-million dollars.

"Turn here!" yells June.

I turn left on Lyons, lakebound again. Up here, the street pattern is almost perfectly arranged north-south, east-west: a rare thing in New Orleans. I feel best in this part of town where I know the cardinal directions: where I know which way to look toward Tennessee. Lyons is slightly off north-south, one of those streets that fills in an angle. It merges with Upperline Street, which we crossed on Annunciation, about ten blocks north of Wisner Park. It does not re-emerge hopefully in the distance—it just ends.

"That's where the Egyptians live," June mentions, as we pass a corner-store house.

"They cured me of my cancer," he says. "I was very sick, about to die. They made herbal medicine for me, and it worked.

"Turn here!" he yells and I head downtown-bound on Magazine Street. He is yelling because he keeps forgetting he is in the car riding with someone who is unfamiliar with New Orleans—who will take Annunciation too far and get to the one-way part, who will continue all the way to Napoleon on these backstreets instead of going up to Magazine or worse, will go the other way to Tchoupitoulas Street—the exact opposite direction of where we are going—and then go all the way down to Napoleon. I get the sense June has not ridden with someone who does not know his way around, in a very long time. So the directions come at the last minute, at high volume, as we make our way.

We go to the pawnshop on Magazine Street by Breaux Mart, to June's mother's house on Louisiana Avenue Parkway. We go across the Industrial Canal to a community center in the Lower Ninth Ward, to the French Quarter, to Marrero on the West Bank. Often I am in a neighborhood where I would be lost—or even in danger—but for June in the passenger seat. With his hanging braids and searching eyes and knowledge of the streets, he is the perfect balance to my blissfully unaware, resident tourist staring at the sky, looking for parakeets.

One time we were trying to give his cousin a ride but missed him and had to do some backing up and going around for construction, until June was about fed up. I went the wrong way for a couple of blocks on a one-way street and some people yelled and gestured from a front yard. June and I waved and smiled and said we're sorry but kept going, there being just one lane between the parked cars and no place to turn around.

We pulled over somewhere in Broadmoor and it seemed like a nice spot. There was a big gathering in a front yard not far down the street. It was a beautiful day for a party. As we pulled into the spot we passed some men sitting in a car. I parked in front of them and started watching the party down the street.

June was craning his neck. "I don't like the look of these guys, wait here," he said.

He got out and went to the car behind us and spoke

through the passenger's window for a moment. He came back to my car.

"It's a good thing I got out, they was ready to shoot," he said.

"Shoot!" I said. "What?"

"They had their guns out. They was watching that party and thought we might be a threat. Here, let's pull around this corner."

***

Some time later we are leaving Pastor Will Walker's Noah's Ark Missionary Baptist Church on South Saratoga Street in Central City. Pastor Will runs a food pantry, and we are here to pick up food for one of June's neighbors: an elderly woman struggling to raise a houseful of children in her care for one reason or another. Mass incarceration is a national crisis that has hit hardest in black neighborhoods, removing criminals, but also sons and fathers. June doesn't waste any time after hearing about the lady. He finds out about her need, he knows somebody else who can help, and he gets on the move putting the two together. At June's urging Pastor Will gave me an oversized bag of dog food, enough to feed my two dogs for a month. It sits in the back beside June's guitar in the coffin case, which we have also just picked up. All this is going on, but June keeps a tight focus on the guitar.

"I had this guitar when I was young," he says. "I went to Will and he gave me this guitar—it was red. But first, he had a Les Paul. So I get the Les Paul and I perform with it. And I bring it back, like this. So I went back to get the Les Paul for a gig, same case, but when I opened it up, it was this." He indicates the guitar in the back: an Epiphone, pearl-white, with a tiny gold ghost hand screwed into the head between the tuning keys, the palm open and the fingertips reaching for the audience.

"I said to Will, 'Where you got that from?' He said, 'A man came in, told me to give you this. He said he was your daddy.'

"I said, 'My daddy's dead, bruh.'

"He said, 'He left it here. An old man brought it, and said give it to you, this is my son's.'

"And I wanted it so bad. And when I opened it up, it was the same guitar that I had when I was fourteen years old, just a different color. You hear me, bruh? I couldn't believe it.

"The case stands up by itself."

June Meets Dog

June was there for a talent show at Hays Chicken Shack.

"It was a lot of people, with a lot of different talents. It was on Louisiana Avenue," says June. "My dad brought me, and Dog's mom brought Dog. His name was Preston Adams. And I went up and done my part for the talent show. I played. And then this little guy got on a trap set, and started playing. Man, he was bad. When Dog got through I went to my dad and said, 'I like that drummer.' He said, 'You do?' I said, 'Yeah.' So dad left and he brought Dog and his momma, introduced us, and we've been together ever since.

"He was real sharp—crazy though! And I don't know why I called him Dog. But I just felt he was my Dog.

"We started hooking up and practicing and doing things. And we did that for a good little while. Man, he was funky.

"I finally left St. Monica, and went to Green. We was like, almost fourteen years old. And that's when Dog said, 'We need to try to do something.' So at fourteen years old he wound up with this girl, and had a little boy named Kenny, so we're running together, and he said, 'Man I'm leaving home.' And I said, 'Wow, let's get up!'

"So he went and got a little place on Peniston Street, in the back. We would just hang up in there and fool around with the music. Girls at school—at Green—

would play hooky there. Then we went to Cohen, and the girls were coming in, and we were up there shedding."

First Bourbon Street Job

"I took a job in the French Quarter—my first job. It was with Chris Owens, at the 809 Club, at Bourbon and St. Louis.

"I had a girlfriend in junior high, at Cohen, her name was Vicky Roach. She was a majorette, a real nice girl. Her daddy was a gambler who lived in Long Beach, California, a pool shark, called Minnesota Fat. And that was his only daughter. She was living down here in New Orleans with her mom, and she was my girlfriend, and one day she said, 'June, you're good on guitar. Why don't you let me hook you up?' I said, 'How you going to do that?' So she called her dad. And I talked to him on the phone. About two weeks later he told me to go to an audition for Sol Owens. And Sol Owens winded up being Chris Owens' husband. So I went in there and I auditioned.

"I wasn't scared. I went in there with a friend of mine. He was a bass player, an older man. Richie. I called him Goose. So we auditioned and that's when he sat us down and he said, 'I tell you what, I can't use the guitar player, but I could use the bass player.' And Goose said, 'June can play bass, too. I already have a job. Why don't you take him as a bass player?' (Sol) said 'O.K.'

"I didn't audition for the bass. He took his word. A few days after that he called, 'Come on down.' And I sat in on the bass for a performance and he liked me. The next day he took me shopping and he bought me a bass guitar."

June had never performed with a bass guitar—just casual, occasional practice.

"But I figured I could play it. And you know, he bought me a Violin-type, the new model, bass guitar. He bought me a wardrobe with shoes, and neckties, and suits, and everything, to wear every night. He told me, 'I'm gonna call you Easy Money. And you'll never wear nothing in life but suit and tie.'

"So I was playing bass behind a guitar player named Lonnie: the hottest guy on Bourbon Street. White boy. Played solo. He had a nice style. We had Gene Man, Clarence Smith on drums. Sometimes Christopher Cruzato, who was Chris' personal drummer. And everything was going pretty smooth.

"Sol Owens was the owner, and he was having trouble with his guitar player. Lonnie was very arrogant. He was around my age at the time. He was a very arrogant guy. And Sol had done bought him a home, and took good care of his children, and this guy was very ungrateful.

"He was so ungrateful, and he thought no one could take his place. He was always wanting more money. He was always riding Sol for more money, and this and that going on.

"And Sol told me one day, 'I want you to learn everything you can learn about this guy. Get his style. And get ready.' So I did. I recorded his style and was practicing on it. I was playing bass behind the same songs that I was gonna play on guitar anyway. So that was no problem. I was learning it all along. It went on like that a while.

"So Lonnie had a habit of coming in late. Sol wants

you onstage for nine, and he means nine. And Lonnie would come in at five after nine. And it came to nine o'clock one day. Sol said, 'Easy money, where's your guitar?' I said, 'It's behind the bar.' He said, 'Strike it up!' "

June was still a minor, suddenly promoted to lead guitar in an adult club. "They didn't care," he said.

"So he called up a guy named T-Man on bass. I took the stage with the guitar, and Sol looked at me playing, and looked at the people, and he went to smiling, and when Lonnie came in through the door he cursed him out, 'You dirty so-and-so, turn around and don't ever come back to my club.' And Lonnie was saying, 'Man, what is going on?' And Sol threw him out of the club.

"So now I'm the guitar, I'm the top guy," June says. "Lonnie started falling. He lost his home, his car, his wife left him. He didn't have Sol no more. And Lonnie came in one night. Sol seen he was in trouble. Sol turned around and looked at me and said, 'Easy Money, do you need a bass player?' I said, 'I think I could use one.' He told Lonnie, 'Get on the bass.' Hired him on the bass. And Lonnie was playing bass behind me. When I started playing bass behind Lonnie! So Lonnie wanted to play guitar, and I knew he was hurtin'. So I said, 'Let's switch up sometime.' And Lonnie got on guitar. And Sol seen him on guitar and ran up there and said 'Didn't I tell you -!' So Lonnie had to give the guitar back.

"But they had some rules. Sol sat me down and said, 'Easy Money, you can stay here forever but let me tell you something: I have rules in this club. Do not have anything to do with the girls. These dancers: Have nothing to do with them. Come in, play your guitar, and there it is.' "

Getting Paid

"At fourteen years old I was playing music. A guy named Larry played drums, picked me up. He was playing with a guy called Butter Bean. These guys would hang in places like a club called Robin Hood, juke joints. And they liked me. Butter Bean had a record of not paying musicians. Certain musicians, he would run off and leave them. But he never done that to me. I tell you that."

June knew how to collect his money. It was a lesson learned from Wilson, Sr., whose friends and son called him "Vic," never Wilson.

Vic helped various people around town as what June calls a porter. It sounds like Vic could wash your car, cut your grass, run an errand or chew your errant teenager out until he straightened out, among many other things. He worked for a number of wealthy and influential people around the city. Vic was supposed to be paid once a month, and he started having trouble getting his money from a certain lady.

So he drove over to her house with June in the truck, and sent June to the door.

"That lady treated me so cold," June recalls. She threw the bill he presented back in his face and slammed the door.

"She didn't answer the door," he told Vic when he got back in the truck.

So they came back the next day. Again, Vic sent June

to the door.

June didn't knock. He went back to the truck and told a lie.

"Nobody home," he said.

Not one to give up, Vic took June back a third time.

"I faked again," says June. "I didn't want the lady to treat me like that."

This time when he got back to the truck and told the same lie Vic got out and went to the door, knocked, and after some aggravated conversation, collected his money.

"He came back with the money and said, 'Here, June,' and gave me the money. He said, 'Don't ever be afraid to get your money.' And he pulled off.

"I turned into a beast after that."

It was no trouble, anyway, to collect from Butter Bean.

"I worked for Butter Bean and Larry, and different things. He had a girlfriend named Cherie, she was real famous, a singer. I had a good time before I ran into Chris Owens and them. That was good experience.

"Me and Dog got into a group called Soul Optimistic. It was Mike Christopher on bass, Greg Adams on keyboard, Joe Francis singing. Joe sounded like Al Green. They had a drummer named Vincent Morehead. But they were having drummer trouble and I told Dog about it. Dog and me were the young guys. It was a band that wasn't hitting on nothing. But the drummer and the guitar style, we turned that band out to number one, and we ran with that a while. We went to another level. We were playing Hunt's Upstairs, Magazine Street clubs. That was a part-time thing I was doing, at the same time as working with Chris Owens late at night. I was doing that on my off days."

Mike Christopher

Mike Christopher is seventy-six years old when interviewed in September 2019; June's elder by about six years. He recalls recruiting June to his Soul Optimistic band.

He had been working with another guitar player named George, but George played strictly rhythm. Christopher needed a lead guitar and was always looking for one. Christopher, a mechanic, happened to work on Vic's car, and the two discussed Christopher's situation. Ever June's promoter and supporter, and remembered by June as much friend, as father, Vic recommended June for the band.

"That cat can play a guitar," says Christopher. "If he can't do nothing else, and I don't know what else he can do, he can play a guitar. If I were to start playing again, I would be looking for June."

By playing he means clubs. He still plays bass, or looks forward to playing, in church. Christopher came up in church. He says, "I was raised so we'd get up and go to Sunday school, after Sunday school go to church, after twelve go home and eat, then go back to church and be there 'til seven or eight at night."

Christopher moved from Mississippi to New Orleans and never stopped being a Christian but he got away from church a little bit. His wife was a pastor at their church for fourteen years and he is still dreaming about finding a site and building a church, or perhaps renovating the old one. He recalled seventeen years playing rock 'n' roll, spending Friday and Saturday night drinking and going to church on Sunday. Christopher came to the conclusion that he had to quit drinking and playing clubs or quit going to church so he let rock music alone.

Recently he has played in the church band—with three women and two men singing, with his daughter on the keyboards, his grandson on the drums, his son-in-law also on drums, while he plays the bass. He is suffering a little bit of gout but he still has his bass and feels like he can still play. "You ain't got to add all that funk, to church music," he says.

Asked to recall some of the places he played, Christopher mentioned Thibodaux, Louisiana; Bourbon Street; Hunt's Upstairs at Washington Avenue and LaSalle—another place called Big Mary's Lounge.

"We were all doing good work," he said. He played with June for years and rehearsed every Monday, often two times a week to get everything together. "Nobody missed," he said.

When June formed the Bayou Band and wanted to go on the road Christopher had to back out.

"I let them have the band," he said. "I was the manager, but I had a wife and children and the other guys wanted to go to Texas. They wanted to leave town. None of them had a wife. But I had a wife and six children and I wasn't going to take them to Texas where I didn't know how we would get along. I had a job every day, and a family."

He remembers good times with June and Joe Francis and Dog, and Greg Adams. They did have some trouble out of an organ player. He was good but drank too much and when he got lost they would just let him sit there at the keys until he could find a way back in. "We just played around him," Christopher says.

He recalls a life of auto mechanics and music, his regular work beginning at eight every weekday at the body shop for forty-five years. "Five o'clock in the evenings I'm taking off and going home, sometimes we'd play Tuesday, Wednesday, Thursday, Friday and Saturday night—and on Bourbon Street on Sunday," he says. He spent four years on contract working Bourbon Street. He had a break most Mondays.

He had no argument with June in the years they worked together.

Christopher and June sometimes played together at the 809 Club. Besides playing at her club Christopher also worked on Chris Owens' Mercedes at the body shop. He has not seen Owens since Hurricane Katrina in 2005, but remembers how good she looked and how hard she worked. He said working the 809 Club, the band had to play for the dancers. They could not go off on their own but needed to pay attention and play things the dancers could work with. They couldn't play any new stuff. They played for the dancers who worked the bar tops.

"Me and June, Greg, Joe, Dog—we all had a good time," Christopher says.

***

June picks up the story about Soul Optimistic.

"We were playing in clubs up around Magazine Street, back in that area; we played with older guys. And they was rough. These guys were con men, cutthroats. But they had our backs, because they were the older guys, and everything. And we learned a lot about them. You know, you get with the old and do what you have to do.

"We hung with it for about three years, but we just overran the group. We were too powerful for them. So that's when I said, 'Hold up, let me put my own thing together.'

He formed the Bayou Band.

"So I got Greg Reddicks, Dog on drums, Geechie (Norwood Johnson) on bass and percussion, a keyboard player, we kept Joe, and we went into a club called Sabou. We started playing. I was doing all originals, Joe was still doing commercial, and we just packed the club. It was hot!"

Dangerous Work

June was working at the 809 Club for Sol Owens but considering going out on his own.

"So people were coming to me making all kinds of offers," he says. "And that's when I knew I had something. But Sol wanted to keep me with Chris. And I don't know if I was moving too fast but I wanted a little more out of life.

"Working Bourbon Street was really dangerous for me. I'll tell you why.

"The girls (in the club) liked Lonnie, they never liked me. And they were trying to find a way to get rid of me.

"Back then I was making ninety-five dollars a week. But he gave me what they called a hustle. I had a hustle. I could do what I wanted in the French Quarter, I could work with girls, help them: girls out there hustling trying to make some money.

"One night I was working in the club and a girl came in. She was standing against the wall, real sexy. She stayed there the whole night. When I knocked off we got together and started talking. She told me, 'Look, I need a little help.' I said, 'What it is?' She said, 'I got like seven girls working for me. I'm having it hard out here with some of these people, and I need you to watch my back.' So I'm trying to figure out what she's talking about. I said, 'I'm not a pimp.'

"She said, 'That's O.K., you know, you're hooked-up. All I need you to do is watch our backs, be there when I need you. And we'll take care of you.' So I went on to her house. It was a penthouse on Royal Street. Big old place. And about seven in the morning the girls start coming in: Six or seven girls come in and start laying money on the table, seven, eight, nine hundred dollars a whop. She said, 'Let's go shopping!' So I went out with them. They took me out, bought me clothes. So I got hooked up with that. That was pretty good.

"I had their backs. And I was making some serious money now. I had seven girls, doing like seven hundred a day, we started buying houses and getting into different things. It was a good life. But I got bored with it. I had a lot of good times in the Quarter. But it got to a point that I just got fed up, man. I needed to try to do my own thing. I had my style.

"So I told Sol, 'Man, I'll give you two week's notice, because I'm moving on.' And he really got pissed. He was like, crazy. He thought I was playing around. So I was playing and he started complaining, 'You're too loud,' and all this. And two weeks was getting close and he called me and said, 'Easy Money, are you really leaving?' I said, 'Yeah, I'm really leaving.' He said, 'I need you to stay with me for about another week until I find someone to take your place.

"He brought me upstairs, gave me some money. And he said, 'You know, we just have to talk about this.'

June never forgot Owens' rule against associating with the dancers in the club. "I was following the rules," he says. But one day some of them joined him at breakfast.

"I was going to breakfast. They said, 'Where you going?' I said, 'I'm going to breakfast at the Downtowner.' The Downtowner was right across the street from where Ernie Vincent is jamming right now. I worked from nine at night to five in the morning, six days a week. And the Downtowner was a hotel and I went in there to get hot chocolate in the morning.

"The girls popped up while I was drinking hot chocolate, three of them, and started saying things like, 'Chris Owens called you this and that,' downed me about being black, was slapping me around, and all this. I started feeling something funny. Next thing I know, I started hallucinating. I knew what it was: LSD. I knew about the LSD high. I was nervous. I had to get away from them 'cause I knew something was going on, and I started looking like I saw my partner on the street. I said, 'Look it's my boy!' and I ran outside. All I could do was flag a cab down to get me where my girlfriend was. I didn't remember the address, but I could get there. 'Just follow my directions!' And he did, he got me there. I slept it off.

"I got back to work that night and Sol called me upstairs. There was like, gangsters standing around. He said, 'We've gotta talk.' He said, 'You were out with some girls, huh?' 'I said, 'Yeah, I was out to breakfast.' He said, 'I heard you wanted to disfigure Ms. Owens.' I said, 'No! What? What's up with that?' He said, 'Well you were with the girls.' I said, 'Yeah, but I was out to breakfast.' He said, 'What went down?' I said, 'These girls were all talking about how Chris Owens called me n-, was cussing me out. I said man, there is something up with that. I got to hallucinating for one thing. They put something in my hot chocolate. I was drinking my hot chocolate and the girls were saying Ms. Owens be cursing and slapping me around and stuff, and they were talking stupid, and saying she was calling me the n-word and all. I started hallucinating. But I'm back now. I came down off that.'

"He said, 'Didn't I tell you I didn't want you socializing with the girls?'

"I said, 'Man, I'm in the restaurant eating, outside the club. I do this every morning.'

"He said, 'What really got to you, what they were saying about Chris?'

"I said, 'They were saying she's calling me all kinds of names, blah blah blah.'

"He said, 'Let me ask you something. If Ms. Owens called you the n-word, what would you do?' I said, 'I don't even worry about that, that's just talk.' He said, 'Well suppose she slaps you?' I said, 'Well, I'm going to give you about ten or fifteen seconds to handle her, or hey, I'll just slap her back.'

"He said, 'Well that's where you make your mistake, Easy Money.'

"I said, 'Oh no no no, let me tell you, Sol, I respect you, but you have to keep your business under control. I play this guitar, I do the best I can, and that's all it is.'

"He said, 'Well let me ask you another question. Why would you want to leave all this—new cars, clothes, house, and all, and get back on the street—going back in the 'hood? I'm asking you from a white man to a brother.'

"And I thought about it. I said, 'Well, to see if I could make it on my own.'

"So he said, 'That's a pretty good reason.'

"He said, 'Look, just go back downstairs and go to work. Start playing. We never had this conversation. I know what I'm fixing to do.'

"And a lot of stuff came out, like foul play, and all of

a sudden some people came around looking for one of those girls. And she wasn't nowhere to be found. I seen posters out there on the strip, looking for a missing person. I just went on and did my usual thing. I didn't get off into it, 'I'm not going to worry about it.'

"So it went on and on for a while."

'When I Turned Violent'

"I used to pay my sister twenty-five dollars a week to get me back and forth to the French Quarter to play music, while she was married to Ernie. We called him 'Sea Dog.' And one night she told me she couldn't bring me, she couldn't go. I said 'Why?' She said, 'He don't want me to go.' I said well put him on the phone. She said he didn't want to talk. ...

"So I knew how Sol was, and I made it to work. I called a cab, and Bourbon Street was so crowded, and I took my guitar and was going through all this. I had to make my money. And I got mad that night and I was at the club.

"Jean Man was the only black drummer that played with Chris. He was a percussion player and a drummer. And that night Jean Man said, 'I got something for you to try.' And it was a tab of acid. But I didn't know nothing about it at the time. I didn't know what it was. He said, 'I want you to try this, but watch it, this stuff is dangerous.' I said, 'This little thing? This is about the size of a pin head.' So I dropped it.

"I started hallucinating. I started thinking about everything that people had done wrong to me in the past. I stumbled by my girlfriend's, she was pregnant, made her get in the car. I had two apartments. I took her to the other one, which I shouldn't have done. I flipped the dresser over and I had a six-point-five carbine rifle. And I said, 'I'm going after my brother in law, who's trying to make me lose my job.'

"I ran out of the house and she screamed. And I was running around Claiborne and First. I ran down Claiborne, turned on Third Street. When I was going down Third Street the police was coming towards me. I was in the middle of the street. And they had their lights on. When they seen what I had, they cut their lights off and put everything in reverse and gave up. They disappeared. I'm still running towards them, but they're gone.

"I made it to Washington Avenue where my sister and her husband were, and I knocked on the door. My sister knew something was wrong. She said, 'What's wrong, June?' I said, 'Open the door, open the door.' She had shutter screens, and she had the wooden door with the glass frame. 'What you got?' When she tried to shut the screen I pulled it open. She broke out and ran. I took the butt and busted the glass, kicked the door open and cranked the gun up. Her husband was standing there. I didn't shoot at first. But when I looked, there were a bunch of Arabs, or whatever they were, coming after me on camels, and they had swords, and it was time to shoot. So I started shooting. I'm blasting away with a six-point-five, one of the most powerful guns you can find, knocking holes through the wall big as a taillight. And my sister got out and ran.

"She was going to my momma's house. And her husband was layin' on the floor. I jumped over him, ran out to the alley, went after my sister. She was running across the park. I was shooting. At that time my mom and dad heard something and they caught me and I went in the house. I didn't know what was going on.

"That's when I turned violent, from that day on. I

really found out what kind of person I was. I'm a good person, and I let things happen, but if I were to get on a certain kind of high or temperament, I would come after you. So I balanced that out. I wouldn't do it like that. I learned if somebody did something wrong in the game, I had patience. I'll wait for a year or two years and then come get you. And that way I can walk away. That's the way street life is, in New Orleans. "A lot of people commit crimes when it comes down to a violent situation, and they do it right then and there. Me myself, unless it's an emergency, I'll just let it go. But don't forget: If you don't come to me sooner or later and straighten it out, I'm coming to get you one of these days—whether it's Christmas, New Year's, or the Fourth of July. Ha ha ha!"

Vera did not know June took acid that night until I told her decades after the incident. She thought he was shooting at Ernie. She never saw June use any kind of drugs and never used them herself. She did not know what a "weed cigarette" was until she was sixty-five.

"He never let me see him do any of that," she says.

She remembers June that night: hiding something behind his back at the door, agitated, coming, she thought, for Ernie. She wanted to run out and meet her brother.

"The Lord told me to go back in," she says. "All of a sudden I heard a boom!"

She saw Ernie on the floor and thought June had shot him. She could not see June's hallucination, of warriors on camels riding in to attack.

"He was sure seeing something, the day he came by that house," she says.

Fifteen Years to Chauffer

Says June, "The cops were looking for me all over for a lot of other things that I had done. One night I told Gene Man, 'I don't think you're going to see me no more because I'm going to have to go to court. And when I go to court, they're going to put me away. All this other stuff is going on.' And Gene said, 'Why you didn't talk to Sol?' I said, 'Talk to Sol? What am I going to talk to Sol for, man?' He said, 'Man you need to talk to Mr. Owens.' And I wouldn't. So he went and ratted. And Sol called me in and said, 'June, when I shut down tonight I want to talk to you.'

"So he shut down that night and said, 'What's going on with you tomorrow?' I said, 'I have to go to court.' He said, 'Who's the judge? You got papers?' I said, 'Yes.' So he took the papers. He looked at me, he said, 'You stupid son of a b-.' He said, 'You see me sitting down tonight with some guys over here?' I said, 'Yeah.' He said, 'That's going to be your judge tomorrow.' I said, 'Wow.' He said, 'I'll tell you what to do.'

"So he wrote a letter, he said, 'Give this to the judge.' And I did. The judge gave me fifteen years. I said, 'Sh-! He don't know what he's doing!' And then they brought me back to court, right after everything was over with, at night. They called me back to trial. I'm in there by myself: Me and the judge and some lady writing down whatever it is, and a guard.

"The judge said, 'Let me ask you something, Wilson.'

He called me Wilson. He said, 'Who are you working for? Do you have a job?'

"I said, 'Sol Owens.'

"He said, 'You need your car?' I said, 'Not really.' He said, 'Well I'm going to take your license. So you won't move around so fast.' He said, 'You got any money on you?' I said, 'I've got twenty-five dollars in my sock.' He said, 'Give me that,' so I gave him the twenty-five dollars. He said, 'When you get to work, give this to Sol.' And he let me free!

"So I got home, my mom and them said, 'What's going on?' So I told her the story. I said, 'He gave me a letter. I'm going to open the letter.' They said, 'Don't open the letter! No, no no!' My dad said, 'That's for Sol!' I said, 'I don't care. It's about me.' So I popped it with a letter opener, and guess what the judge was saying? He said, 'Mr. Owens, I have done everything I could, in my power, to help you with this. But June has been giving a lot of trouble.' He said, 'He's a case. But I hope you appreciate this. It's the best I can do. I'll see you soon.'

"I said, 'Wow, how can a man get a judge to apologize to him, and say this is the best I can do, when I don't have to do fifteen years?' I'm without a driver's license, but I got a chauffer that Sol got, to pick me up and bring me wherever I got to go from now on.

"So he knew I had opened the letter. He just looked at it and went about his business. Sol was the most good, powerful man I have ever seen. People talk about racism, and prejudice. We all have that in us, for certain people. I learned that about Sol. Sol was a racial man, but he treated me like a king, you know what I'm saying? I loved that man. I really did."

Sol and the Money Jar

"Sol Owens really raised me into the game," June recalls. "I wouldn't have known nothing about how to operate on the street, if it wasn't for Sol."

June recalls running into a friend of Owens' who went to school with him. The friend shared a story about Owens running a homework operation back in school, with a nerd doing the homework at Owens' house. According to the story, Owens took fifty cents from the kids at school for the homework assignment, and gave the nerd ten cents.

"Ha ha ha," June laughs.

Then he tells a story about seeing Owens, who could have been considered a wealthy man, going around the block in the French Quarter picking up coins off the street. June said, 'What is going on? Why are you picking up coins out of the gutter?'

Owens said, "Come and let me show you something," and took June upstairs into his apartment. He opened up a closet in the back and there was a jar there, a very tall glass jar full of money—with all kinds of money inside.

Owens pointed out large bills and wristwatches amid the change. It looked like thousands of dollars and a lot of nice stuff.

"Ten years of walking around the block, five times a night, that's what you get," said Owens, as June recalls.

Owens said it was about time to get another jar.
  "I loved that man," says June again.
  Sol Owens died in 1979.

A Guitar Case Full of Acid

"One night I was playing in the club, and a guy said, 'Tonight when you go home, leave your guitar behind the piano bar, just take the case home.' So I did. I was living with a lady, Lillian, all in all we had three kids—she had two when I met her—and when I popped the case open when I got home it was, man, a whole case of acid, LSD, packaged in there. My girlfriend said, 'Wow, what is this?' I said, 'Man, I don't know, what are we going to do with this?' I'm not making that much money. But Sol hooked her up. Her rent was like eight dollars a month. She was getting food stamps. I mean, we were doing O.K. So I went back to the Quarter and put the word out about this LSD hit. One night a guy came in and said, 'Man, look, I can move it.' So I was making money on that end. But I wanted to get out of that."

Cabbage Alley

Hey, Cherie, somebody's got to pay.
Hey, Cherie, somebody's got to pay.
Cheyenne Hunters coming, I know they wanna play.
They gonna come out Mardi Gras Day, oh yeah.
I bet you five dollars, put your money on the flo'.
Somehow, they won't show. Oh yeah.

-June Victory and The Bayou Renegades, 'Cherie'

"I got hooked up with a guy, wanted me to go to the park. He said, 'We're putting a little organization together. Let's do some things in the park. We want you to come out here and help us.' And that was Cabbage Alley. That was a place at Philip and LaSalle, where we would go on Sundays, and let it all hang out."

Cabbage Alley, called Van McMurray Playground on Google Maps, not mentioned on my paper map, is a pocket park between Jackson Avenue and Philip Street in the Central City neighborhood of New Orleans. It has a concrete stage, covered by a star-shaped frame for lighting, with an area for bleachers nearby. There is surrounding grass, some chain-link fencing, and an old basketball court. It is behind a big brick building.

There is no telling when June will show up to walk the Cabbage Alley stage, alone or with some visitor, and dream. We stopped there several times together. At other times, June would point, almost wave to Cabbage Alley as we passed. "I used to own all of this," he tells me one day while standing on the stage, with a broad stretch of his arms indicating the park, significant buildings, and perhaps the whole city surrounding. He remembers the health clinic in the front and in back: a moneymaking party every Sunday. In this city of dreams and dreamers June may be the biggest dreamer of all: a man approaching seventy wanting to pack this park with music and people in the same way he did in 1973. And him ravaged by two or three kinds of deadly maladies, too skinny by the weight of a good-sized dog, smoking nine-dollar-a-pack menthol cigarettes and telling it all to an unknown writer from a small town in Tennessee, as though I might help. Diminished he may be in some ways but June still dances and plays with the guitar on stage, adding superfluous and countless strings of notes behind the tune he carries out front like a vivid banner. He can play rhythm guitar or lead guitar or in a pinch, both. He can talk and tell stories in such an entertaining way a person wants to be a part of June's dream. If guitar picking and politicking can get it done, June can do it.

When they called June to help with Cabbage Alley, the neighborhood was different: packed with people, for one thing. New Orleans' population peaked around 1960. The South Claiborne Avenue corridor, a few blocks lakeside of Cabbage Alley, was lined with clubs and you could not fit another person on the sidewalks, or on the dance floors, on a Saturday night. That's the way June recalls it. There were enough music lovers here to support a myriad of juke joints and an outdoor venue, which Cabbage Alley became. Then economics and the drug trade, joblessness and gun violence, hurricanes and hopelessness depleted the neighborhood of people and opportunities. These backstreets and avenues are still home to many thousands, though, and hopeful signs are present: including renovated, colorful homes all through these blocks. The city skyline rises dramatically to the east and the Superdome is just a five-minute drive from here. But the online news outlet Uptown Messenger reported recently that Central City has become a "food desert," after the closure of the Dryades Public Market grocery store. So the news is mixed.

"I went to Cabbage Alley that Sunday," June recalls, thinking almost fifty years back down the line of memories. "I set up the sound, and it was rolling, man, Sunday in the day time. In the evening we had to go to Sabou and play. I was working another club on Orleans Street called Cynthia's. I met Phil Johnson and Oscar Cage, and they went to Werlein's (music store) and got all kinds of equipment, fifty, sixty thousand dollars worth of equipment. And trucks to haul it with. I put everybody on salary. So we're running around, and then I'm hooking up with Tipitina's trying to do some stuff.

"Then we went to the Parisian club, right across from Cabbage Alley, and were jamming there. I had the Bayou Band. A guy named Joe Drummond had a liquor store in the club. He was out of L.A. He just wanted to give it up. He hired a guy, named Theo, and Theo wasn't paying him rent, saying this and saying that. He'd just lost the business.

"So I was on the road, playing around. I went into Tracy Knight's studio, cut a song called 'One More Silver Dollar,' and 'Down On the Bayou.' I was doing 'One More Silver Dollar' live. And just putting it out, playing, playing, playing. And I wound up getting caught up with Gregg Allman, because I knew Peter Frampton. I was running around with all these groups from out of town. I started hearing this song called 'Midnight Rider,' and I thought, 'Wow.'

That was June's song on the radio, musically different but most of the lyrics intact.

He has never known how The Allman Brothers Band got the song, though. He has never seen a penny from it, and nobody ever asked for it. Decades after this timeframe, a 2019 Wikipedia search suggests June's manager for part of his career, Allison Miner, had been in a Daytona Beach, Florida high school band with Duane and Gregg Allman called A. Miner & the Allman Joys. If true, that's a pretty strong connection to a band June never played with despite their frequent visits to New Orleans.

When I tell June about this Wikipedia information he appears thunderstruck for a moment, and then clams up. We later talk about it again and he has been discussing it with his friend and confidante Ernie Vincent. He says Ernie, a master of intellectual property rights, was pragmatic about it. June wouldn't have had the money to take "One More Silver Dollar" to the top of the charts.

"They done me a big favor, they showed me I could write a hit record," says June.

He says Ernie Vincent told him, "They made us famous, brother."

June says of his former manager, "She was watching to get more music. But they only got that one song. At that time, it was over. That song is all they got. But it was one of the good ones."

June says he wrote the song in a Metairie hotel room where he was hiding out. He arrived in a rush, feeling hunted.

"I threw the stuff in my pockets on the dresser, there in the hotel room, my keys and stuff. It was a silver dollar in there, and a little bit of loose change.

"Later, I sat down and wrote that song."

I ask June why he never filed a lawsuit over "One More Silver Dollar"—to reclaim his lyrics, at least.

"I liked the way they done it," he says. "And they never came back to sue me. I put my version out, why they didn't sue me? Nobody wants the song to die."

It reminds him of the song, "Old Time Indian": "Old time Indian like to drink, like to fight, but everybody is trying to be friends, because nobody wants to die."

He never wrote for money, anyway: "You write for the rich, for the homeless, the broke. That's what it's about."

While all this was going on June was busy—and about to confront potential big-time trouble.

"At the Parisian Room this guy said, 'I'm having some problems with this club and if I could get you to pack the place, it might work out. I'll give you so much of the register. Pay you like two hundred a night.' So I came to town, got a bunch of girls together, and we had a reunion and packed the club. He said, 'I want you to hang with me, while I get this thing back together.' I said, 'O.K., but I'm not paying hotel bills. Some of these people are not from here.' So he said, 'O.K.' He said, 'I've got a place in the back.' I packed the club, making money for the dude. He claimed he was going to give me twenty-five percent off the register, plus the salary. So he wasn't feeding me the register, which was cool, because we were having fun, and we were doing Cabbage Alley on Sunday. We were getting to be like twenty-four, twenty-five now. And I took sick one night. Really had the flu. I couldn't make it.

"Next thing I know he took all the equipment, man. The girls are calling, Geechie's on the phone, saying, 'Hey man, this guy's taking the equipment, saying all this,' crazy. And I said, 'Hold up, man, get the girls out of there. This guy's tripping.'

"So the next day I went down there. I was looking for him. I stayed around there 'til about two that morning. He pops up. We go in the back. He's got the guitar equipment and some other stuff. Tells me I owe him some money.

"He said, 'Hey, did you tell the guys I've been paying you some money under the table?'

"And one of the guys jumps up, I think it was Norwood, he said, 'Man, we're not worried about that.' Which he was. I split the take with the group. I said, 'How much we owe you?' He said, 'A hundred dollars.' So I stuck my hand in my pocket. I was broke. I said, 'Let me see the stuff.' So he took us out to the parking lot, popped his trunk open. I seen he had a pistol in his waistband. He was talking crazy. So I put my hand out behind me. Someone put a pistol in my hand. And I just drawed down on him. 'Come on man, give me my stuff.' This was crazy. But that's the way New Orleans is.

"Theo was dangerous, yeah. He had done shot seven people. Kilt five.

"I took his gun away from him. He got down on his knees and started begging for his life. Something told me, 'Don't let him go.' He was begging too much. He scared me."

June imagined some of those seven people had begged Theo to spare them.

"I liked the guy. I didn't want to see him die, with his eyes looking at me," says June. He told Theo to get up, to "die like a man." Then he told him to get out of there.

"When he got up to walk away I shot him in the back," June says. "I shot him with his own pistol.

"I took his gun, brought it to Joe Drummond, his landlord, told him what happened. Next thing I know they've got an attempted armed robbery, attempted murder charge on me. It turned out all kinds of bad for me. I wound up in jail."

Theo was hospitalized but recovered.

"I called him from jail and told him he'd better try to do something about the charges," June says. "He didn't know I was in jail."

June's dad and other family members saw Theo after the shooting. Theo was asking for a payoff, June says.

One day Vic saw Theo in the barbershop. "When Theo walked out to walk away, somebody killed him," June says. "I didn't have anything to do with that. He had a lot of enemies."

June pleaded self-defense to his charges, evading a possible prison sentence when the jury ruled in his favor.

"All that passed over and we was working in Kenner one night. I told Dog, 'You know what this band needs? A harmonica player. On the real.' And we were sitting down outside the club, on the ground, and a guy opened the door to the hotel, 'Can I sit in with you?' And we said, 'What do you play?' He said, 'Harmonica.' That was Bob Turner. Man, we were ready now.

"We had Robert Turner on harmonica, Greg Reddicks on bass, Dog on drums, me on guitar. I kept Joe Francis as a commercial singer. I got Twiggy from the Grateful Dead on guitar, and I wound up with

Lawrence, the keyboard player out of SUNO, and we hot as a firecracker.

"So we're booking all over Louisiana. Nonstop. Packing the house. Then we ran into Jackie Wilson, 'Danny Boy.' He said, 'Man, I need this group in the Sunrise!' So now I'm working for Jackie Wilson in the Sunrise. Next thing I know I'm working with Pure Ice, Mcfadden & Whitehead, The Bar-Kays, The Manhattans—and we're moving."

Ernie Vincent

He is in the Louisiana Music Hall of Fame and took home a Lifetime Achievement Award from New Orleans' *OffBeat Magazine* in 2013. He is a blues guitarist who loves jazz and country. But most of all Ernie Vincent, "hittin' seventy" in 2019, is a bandleader. A resident of New Orleans East, he has played the John F. Kennedy Center for the Performing Arts in Washington, D.C., and has been overseas many times.

"But I have to have the band that can go, you understand?"

He explains that playing one of his songs can take months of arrangement, the rhythm section, which Vincent writes, practicing together and the horn section, another writer's job, practicing together until each unit has its part down, and they can merge and work it out.

"I could travel right now anywhere in the world, if they could get the horn section together. If I could play 'Dap Walk,' that's all it takes," says Vincent.

"Dap Walk" is his 1972 song, a hit for two years before he knew it was a hit, arising out of a time when he and his Top Notes band were watching the bass player, Dap, walk through the room like his feet were broken.

"That was the way he walked," Vincent recalls. "He couldn't walk barefooted. He was a good friend of mine. And he was a good bass player. He was one of the best I ever had. He was from Kenner.

"That band wasn't six months old when I did that,"

says Vincent.

It has lasted more than forty years.

"Dap Walk" is an instrumental groove in Ernie Vincent style, that is, Chicago-influenced, strong-on-horns blues with a zydeco rhythm. It begins with Vincent's plea, "Hey, get up brother! Do any dance that's groovy to you!"

"Zydeco is all about two-step music. That's why people dance on everything we do," says Vincent.

"I get a kick out of writing and creating," he says. "It's amazing to intellectually create something, put it on paper, teach them to sing it, and then go in the studio and record it."

He describes himself as "driven," always working two or three jobs. "I was always afraid to have just one job," he says.

He has lived a clean life.

"I always led people. Therefore, I had to stay on top of everything. I've always had that leadership ability, and I think it's because I had a drive."

Vincent's father played guitar and harmonica. Vincent built his first guitar himself. He made his first amp out of his mother's little radio, after figuring out how to create a clear channel and wire-in his guitar. He might have been an electrician. He was born in New Orleans and attended Booker T. Washington High School, but he also lived in Thibodaux where his family is from. He and his wife of forty years made sure their children had a college education.

In New Orleans, he lived uptown in the old days and listened to Bobby "Blue" Band, James Brown, and Kool and the Gang. He remembers the older folks getting together and making music "back of town, drinking their corn liquor and stuff, and the wife would be cooking gumbo. Musicians from all over the country would try to find those places and get some of that corn liquor and good food.

"I would go over there just strumming, jamming guitar with them," he says.

He says, "Uptown was nice." He remembers Indians coming out of the alley hollering. He remembers an old lady named Miss Sally. "She used to sell weed and wine," says Vincent. "I wrote a song called 'Pork Chop Alley.' It's about that lady.

"When we Uptown, we all get down, Pork Chop Alley," he sings into the phone.

He remembers the music at Cabbage Alley. It was not far from his house on First Street, by Philip Street where the park is.

"I remember the band playing and man, I didn't know who it was. I didn't know June at the time."

It was on Bayou Lafourche that opportunity knocked for Vincent. He was practicing guitar, loud "as always," in Thibodaux one day when a Creole drummer rolled up in a Cadillac.

"He said, 'Man, we want you to come play with us," Vincent recalls.

"I said, 'I just know three songs.'

"He said, 'That's plenty.' "

So Vincent had his first gig in Bridge City, Jefferson Parish, at the Shangri La, with "people packed in there." He did his three tunes including something by Muddy Waters. "You sang what you felt like in those days," he says.

"I said, 'You know what, I have to get better,' " says Vincent, so he went to Houston music school, and eventually played Tony's club at Grand Isle around the same time as June Victory. Their paths crossed so many times, but they did not meet until the mid-1980s.

Vincent says Joe Tex and others he met in Grand Isle wanted him to go with them on the road. "I said, 'I can't, I gotta hold my band together.' If it weren't for me being loyal to the band, I would have been gone a long time ago. But I'm glad I was that way. I might have been dead."

Vincent describes his music as "strictly old-school, backwater blues."

He remembers riding the overnight bus to Nashville to record 45s. He has written over two hundred songs and played with all the New Orleans Indians. He played a year and nine months with Chris Owens on Bourbon Street. "I caught two Mardi Gras with her," he recalls.

"Famous people come in and sit in with her," says Vincent. "You can learn a lot. They got a lot of talented people in New Orleans."

He played the New Orleans Jazz & Heritage Festival fifteen years in a row. He is also a promoter and producer with his own label, Kolab Records, Inc. He recorded June and produced The Bayou Renegades' *Matsue House Party*, in 1996, on which Vincent also had several songs. He is currently excited about recordings he has of a number of musicians, including the late Ernie K-Doe, Mathilda Jones, "one of the best female vocalists here in New Orleans," and Tommy Singleton. "Tommy knows a lot of songs," says Vincent.

He describes his lifestyle as "working and gigging, working and gigging."

When he needs a guitar player fast, he knows one he can call. "I have called June at the last minute: 'June, I need you for so-and-so.' June said, 'Where do you want me?' I said, 'Well, meet me at the airport at nine in the morning.' "

"We feel like we're related," says Vincent.

The Deep Freeze and Other Business

June shares a short story:

"I ran into this guy who wanted to get in the cigarette business. My cousin came and said, 'We got this guy wants to invest. How much do you think he needs, June?' I said, 'If he can come up with like a bill, that's a hundred thousand, to match what we got, I think we can do some business.' "

"Man, this guy lived in a raggedy house and next thing I know, he opened up a deep freeze and there the money was!"

There were many business ventures—call them adventures—along the way. Subject as he was to misfortunes with labels and regrettable decisions like putting his foot down over production details, keeping his pride but losing a record deal, June stopped playing guitar in public. He was involved in banking outside the regulatory scheme, and other forms of gambling. He did some amount of drug dealing. He was a collection agent and an effective one—but that did not last long due to his empathetic nature.

He tried the shrimp business, on the shore-side. He remembers buying shrimp for fifty cents a pound and selling them in St. Louis, Missouri for eight dollars a pound. The deal was so good June invested in a 1965 International Loadstar with two freezers in the back and a generator on the running board. It was a U.S. Post Office truck with the look of authority and they went "fast, fast" along the highway pumping shrimp water out into the road along the way. He moved about two thousand pounds of shrimp and remembers getting them from Vietnamese shrimpers on Lake Pontchartrain.

"They were coming with the boat all day and all night," he says. "It was like a challenge. We told the guy at the office we were picking it up for the bishop at the church. And he would give them to us for like fifty cents. We would come back to the church on Sunday and have a shrimp deal, and sell them for like a dollar a pound. So we were donating back to the church. Isn't that something?"

He found his stride in mudjacking: leveling and fixing cracked concrete slabs, and reinforcing foundations in the tricky New Orleans soil. He knows a lot about soils. It is not easy to resolve foundation issues in south Louisiana. There is not much rock material and water lurks everywhere. It requires a lot of drilling and digging and involves a lot of mud, and no small amount of ingenuity.

"You use a concrete pump called a MJ-10, they use it to pump concrete. It's a small pump. But what I done with it, instead of pumping concrete, I put mud in it," he says. "In New Orleans, there's a lot of voids, it's void under these houses, a lot of these brick houses. So I would connect a hose to the mud pump, wash mud, it was humus, garden soil, and pump it under the house to put the soil back."

He could also level driveways or sidewalks.

"That was a new thing. I went into that business. I'd take a rotor hammer, two-inch bit, and drill through the slab, like the size of a tennis ball, and let's say if the slab's six feet, I would put towards the end a hole on each end, and in the center. So while it's pumping I'm watching it as it's coming up and I'm moving from hole to hole to keep it balanced, so it could just come up.

"It was muddy work, real muddy. Especially when you're filling under houses. Mudjacking is not that bad. But when you're filling under houses ...

"I found a new type of soil called red clay. Nobody was fooling with it because they couldn't pump it. But I found a way to pump red clay, red Mississippi soil ... I could get an eighteen-wheeler load for a hundred dollars, when for the humus, it was thirty dollars a yard. So that was a lot of money. I started cutting prices down, so I didn't have competition, because they didn't know how to pump red clay. I was the only one doing it."

June has opinions about everything, including house-raising, common in New Orleans to get homes well above the waterline. He feels like it is crazy to raise your house almost, but not quite high enough to put your car under there and lectures about it whenever we pass such a place.

"The federal government got interested in the mudjacking company. I had the gambling operation. They came in and took over that part of it. They just left me alone. I still would make money with it, though. But they just took it over, the feds. They also took over the gambling operation. They broke up all the f- machines. I looked at it on the news. They went in there with a sledgehammer."

The Internal Revenue Service cleaned June out, and it still haunts him. "They don't let up," he once said about the IRS as we were rolling along under the Napoleon Avenue trees.

He went to a parish prison with only nine inmates "over in Belle Chase" then was urged in a new direction—studying the law under Ellis Pailet and Mary Ann McGrath Swaim.

"They sent me to school for law, but when I graduated, they wouldn't give me a job for the law, because they said I was a convicted felon. But they sent me to school. The federal government. Ha ha."

He never stopped loving his friends and his family. One time he wanted to give his sister something for Mother's Day, but didn't have money to spend and he told her so.

As Vera tells it, "I said, 'I don't need no money. I need you to come by this club where I am going, and I want you to sing 'Walking the Back Street' for me.' It was a song he did, that I loved.

"I didn't know if he was going to come or not," she remembers. "He did show up, and he played! Them people screamed, them people hollered, them people was passing out!

"When he finished I made an announcement on the mic: that this is my brother, and he's sick with colon cancer, lung cancer [three kinds of cancer]. And I asked them to pray for him. And them people started up screaming. It was something pitiful!"

Vic and the Cigar Box

"Anytime a man has something, look behind his back at the woman's he's with. Look at the woman at his back. That's why he has something. If he doesn't have anything- "

-Vera Sterling, retelling one of her dad's favorite sayings

And here is a story about Vic Victorian, who is working the door at a club June is playing back-in-the-day.

He loved his son's music so much. Vera recalls coming home sometimes and finding Vic and June in the back room, June singing Vic's favorite, the broken-heart song "Take Your Chances," which could make a hit on the country charts.

"That song right there will make somebody cry," says Vera.

The club Vic and June are working is having trouble with robbers. June is playing guitar and singing, and Vic is working the door. Vic has a cigar box full of money. He is watching the money, watching June and the customers, probably waiting for June to sing "Take Your Chances."

A robber comes up.

"He pulled out a knife," says June. "Vic opened the cigar box, took the money out and put it in his pocket, and gave the man the cigar box. He said, 'You ain't got the nerve to use that knife.' The man hesitated. And the owners jumped him from behind and threw him out of the club. We left with our money."

Vic Victorian died in 1998.

Wilson Sr. and Mildred Victorian. Vera Sterling Photo

June's First Communion—at about seven years old. Vera Sterling Photo

June Victory. Vera Sterling Photo

June Victory and Vee Fire Queen onstage (undated). Vera Sterling Photo

The Bayou Band—date unknown. From left: Preston Adams aka Dog, Mike Christopher, Joe Francis, Greg Adams, and June Victory. Vera Sterling Photo

Ernie K-Doe, singer Marilyn Barbaran (not mentioned elsewhere in the text), June Victory, and Schelita Sterling (later, Schelita White), at the New Orleans Jazz & Heritage Festival, 1989. Vera Sterling Photo

Funky 544, Bourbon Street. Brent Andrews Photo

June checks the setlist outside Funky 544. Brent Andrews Photo

Mark Appleford, June Victory, and Tommy Singleton playing Funky 544 as The Mojo Shakers. Brad "Lefty" Keith is behind June (and the screen), on the drums. Brent Andrews Photo

June Victory and Chief Kenny Young out front at Igor's Checkpoint Charlie, Esplanade Avenue. Brent Andrews Photo

Vee Fire Queen on Mardi Gras Day 2018. Brent Andrews Photo

Big Chief "Little Walter" Cook of the Creole Wild West, seen over June Victory's shoulder on Mardi Gras Day. Brent Andrews Photo

June Victory and Vee Fire Queen with The Bayou Renegades at Bamboula's theater on Frenchmen Street, late 2019. Amy Geszvain Photo

Vee Fire Queen on Mardi Gras Day 2019. Brent Andrews Photo

Mildred Victorian's house. Brent Andrews Photo

The Bayou Renegades

Me and my Spyboy, gon' take 'em running.
Indians, jumping and running.
Big Chief, dressed in blue,
See my Flag Boy, he know what to do.
Spyboy, dressed in white, got 'em boy, out of sight.
Pretty White Eagle, I say pretty White Eagle.
Uptown ruler, I say Uptown ruler.
Wild Magnolia, I say Wild Magnolia,
Hundred & One, gon' have some fun.

- June Victory and the Bayou Renegades, 'Hold 'em Joe'

June was in trouble, but he could get out of it by taking his south Louisiana sound out of town. It was not the first time. He has been sentenced to fifteen years in prison and thirty years in prison but never spent more than a few days in jail. Somebody always came to him with an offer: Get out of jail and play music, go on the road or live under house arrest in New Orleans, and play music. It sounds unusual, but not to June. He calls it "a regular deal, for certain people." He says, "I live under a different umbrella in New Orleans. The criminal justice system always protected me."

And why not? June playing your town in Tennessee, or Minnesota, or France, can only make you want to go to the place that lit such a flame as he carries. You cannot help but want to see the backstreets and the strip where the player found his pulse. New Orleans lives on oil and tourism. And everybody comes looking for the music they have heard or heard about back home.

June says, "They took me out of jail. They told me to put a band together real fast, and get out of here, and we'll cut you a deal."

June had a special love for sewing music, the traditional songs New Orleans Indians use to help with the long stationary hours beading suits for Mardi Gras, and sing in the streets Mardi Gras Day. June played with the Mardi Gras Indian band the Wild Magnolias; they have been a hit in their Indian suits in New Orleans and around the world. The Wild Magnolias' songs are more traditional than June's guitar-driven rock, the guitar not being an Indian walking instrument. When June and his band combined rock 'n' roll guitar and lyrics about the Indian heroes—Big Chief, Spyboy, Wild Man—they created a musical gumbo people loved.

June recalled a Cheyenne Hunters Big Chief listening to "Don't Rock the Bow," a simple, repetitive song, without much guitar flourish, about an Indian trying to get home. The Big Chief told June he was beading his suit and listening to the song and before he knew it, "I done made a whole row," June recalls with a laugh.

They called June's work "talking and singing at the same time." He was playing in four-four time, "but I'm singing in time-and-a-half. So you can hear every word."

Geechie had been telling June about his idea for a band with just three pieces: guitar, bass guitar, and bass drum. June recruited a youngster, Earl Nunez, for bass, and Geechie shared singing duties with June while playing bass drum.

Dog stopped playing in public.

June was still calling his group the Bayou Band, with new personnel. "I had to change the name," he recalls. "Geechie said, 'Why do that?' I said, 'I don't want nobody to know I'm out there.'

"He said, 'Let's call it The Bayou Renegades,' " June says. They worked on it as a side-gig while they went to Minnesota with the Wild Magnolias, featuring the famous Big Chiefs Bo Dollis and Monk Boudreaux.

They played in the club where Prince filmed *Purple Rain*. Tracy Chapman was playing there at that time, and some associates of the Purple One. Chapman's hit "Fast Car" had everyone out on the road with the windows down.

Working at first as Three Man Crew, June, Geechie and Nunez took The Bayou Renegades idea to the stage in Minnesota. People wondered what kind of act they were about to see. The stage didn't look like much of anything, with no drum kit and the amps tucked underneath.

"We just plugged into the stage. On the stage was just a bass drum," June recalls. But after a few minutes of Three Man Crew/The Bayou Renegades Indian funk, of flying guitar and jumping bass, and Indian characters coming out of the woodwork, "People couldn't believe it. They started jumping off the balcony and everything else."

June soon found a drummer named Jasmin Cardriche and recruited her to round out his act. The music puts the real stories of the Mardi Gras Indians beside scuffling guitar, and over many layers of percussion—tribal songs as stadium rock.

"I took Jasmin and put her with The Bayou

Renegades. She was running with me and the Wild Magnolias," he recalls. "She was from the past, but she wound up playing with me and the Wild Magnolias in France."

His manager, Allison Miner, sent the band overseas.

June recalls good times playing in France and Japan, where June met his Japanese counterpart, June Yamagishi, and they waged an epic guitar battle. There were big crowds and little jet airplanes that took off straight up. June recalled the good times recently during a rare reunion with Earl Nunez in New Orleans.

Arriving in a Japanese city and starving at 4 a.m. local time, they mentioned it to someone and before long the mayor, of all people, had gotten involved and they took the Renegades to a closed restaurant. When they went into the restaurant and saw the workers "all them was lined up, sleepy," like they had been called out of bed and June could tell they didn't like being there that time of morning. The band passed a fish tank on the way in, with a big octopus lurking and reaching. June and the band sat down and ate their fill of delicious, exotic food they could not identify. "On the way out, we passed the fish tank, and the octopus was gone!" June recalls with a laugh.

There were temptations of the flesh on the road, but June took a businesslike approach, avoiding romance and focusing on the music.

Meanwhile business deals still went sour through indifference, incompetence, and sometimes, backstabbing. The Bayou Renegades had that sound, but were not lucky, and so it goes sometimes.

As an example of the tricks played on him in the music business, June recalls that a producer once recorded the Renegades' music and replaced bassist Nunez with a bass track, without telling June about it. There was something wrong with the recording, and everybody was trying to figure it out. June says they brought in outside help to try and fix it, but could not. They brought June in and he listened to the song. He asked for quiet and listened closely.

"I said, 'Put the real bass player in there!' " June recalls.

"They said, 'What? That is the real bass player!' "

June said no, it wasn't, and he could tell because it lacked Nunez's "trademark," a strong pluck of the string that jumps out every eighth or sixteenth note.

That jumping bass is the key to June's brand of Indian funk music and the producer washed it out.

"It didn't make sense, huh?" says June. "So what they plan was? To steal the publishing," he says. "But I caught them."

June once put his foot down about being paired up with Rebirth Brass Band on a potential release, and lost the deal. He had nothing against Rebirth. He just felt it did not fit well with his Indian music. He made his point, but no money.

"That was a mistake," he admits now.

It isn't just labels and producers getting up to tricks; club managers try their share too.

"They get too greedy. And then they go to messing with you," June says. "Trying to work you to death, and stealing at the same time. I've been at it too long. I know all the tricks."

Industry politics and unhappy circumstances brought The Bayou Renegades to a halt. The music remains available here and there on the Internet, not producing any revenue for the musicians. June is now trying to get into the same groove with a number of New Orleans' best players, and is gigging regularly around the city—sometimes just for tips.

'Early in the Morning'

There are secrets in The Bayou Renegades' self-titled, 1998 Monkey Hill Records CD: about the movements of the Indians in New Orleans, about the songs themselves. June says "Hold 'em Joe" and "Runaway Indian" are the same song, played at different speeds, one with words, and one without.

"People never caught on to that," he says.

"Hold 'em Joe" is about the Indians taking to the street behind an angry Big Chief. It thumps and plods along at walking speed. The instrumental "Runaway Indian" drips with style, beginning when Geechie lets the hammer down on the bass drum, then is urged on by Nunez who tries to break a bass string about every eighth or sixteenth note. June's guitar drops in with trickles and rips before settling into a tempestuous flow. What's it all mean? "That's about me," says June, the former runaway Indian who played with the greats as a fourteen-year-old boy in Grand Isle. Through the careful notes and nervous chords and fast-moving bass line I can sense the storms coming in; June would be worried about his tent and his clothes, and perhaps his cash, getting wet. He might or might not be looking forward to another hamburger. I can see jaws dropping in the audience, when the youngster takes the stage and begins working his axe.

We return frequently to a certain time of day on the Renegades' CD: early in the morning. Time is a recurring theme, here. Played for the most part by the Three Man Crew of June, Geechie, and Nunez, the recording includes assists from drummer Cardriche and percussionist Patrick Williams, as well as keyboardist Dwight Cassanova, with voices of many other New Orleans Indians helping out. It leans deep into New Orleans Indian culture for its stories and its characters. It was produced by June and his late friend, Frank Quintini.

The morning theme begins to work its way into the listener's conscience on the first song, "Down On the Bayou," which after its introduction reflective of the Apache Wars earnestly cries "waking up early, getting up early" with a frenetic pace, calling the sisters, brothers, and Spyboys together:

"Ain't no Indian gang, in my way.
We'll be knocking 'em down, early.
Down on the bayou, where we all come from.
Down on 'ey Bayou, that's where we all come from."

The Big Chief declares "getting out early!" and "break it down early!" and:

"Take my arrow, bring no gun.
This time brother, say we won't run.
There's a young generation, not far behind.
There's no need to poison their minds.

Give me a drink of whiskey, I'll let you smoke my pipe.
We'll party, and dance all night.
Gimme 'drink of whiskey, let you smoke my pipe.
And on the battlefield, say 'We won't fight.'

Down on that bayou, where we all come from ..."

However it goes down, it will happen in the morning. The singer declares, "Me start early!" "Starting early!" And, "Indian, are you ready? Indian, better get ready!" And for what? Dancing and partying.

"That's for peace," June says of the song, wanting it so badly for his people and his city.

***

The morning theme kicks off "Hold 'em Joe": "Chief got mad, left early in the morning. Something was going wrong."

Song six, "Early in the Morning," sung by June and his friend Honore, begins:

"Early in the morning when the sun won't shine
I got two pretty Queens and a gallon of wine.
Fifteen stitches across my chest,
I have no fear, and fear no death."

June says this is the Big Chief speaking and he has been out and tangled with a tall Spyboy who left him scarred. One by one, braves come to the Big Chief competing to go after the Spyboy with the ridiculous stature.

"When you're on the street, you're going after certain Indian parties, we're talking about years ago," June says. "You're talking about a Spyboy who is six feet tall and there ain't no way he can be Spy, because everybody can see him. He was too tall to be a Spyboy. Most of our Spyboys would be four feet tall, or a little over.

"The leader is talking, he done been out there, he

done been in a scuffle," says June. "He come back, he get drunk, he ready to go back out there and take care of business."

Confident and among friends, singing braves start saying this enemy may be tall, he may be bad, and yes he has been calling the shots, but he has messed with the wrong people. The braves want to go out with the Big Chief and settle the score. The people start partying and singing "early in the morning" and "early that morning" between the lines of the braves. Sings one brave:

"I seen his shadow!"
"Early in the morning."
"I seen him running!"
"Early in the morning."
"They call him Spy."
"Early in the morning."
"I'll take him down."
"Early that morning."
"He big and tall."
"Early in the morning."
"I know he is."
"Early in the morning."
"I'll make him bow-"
"Early in the morning."
"In shadow water."

Shadow water: water down here in Louisiana, that is covered in the shadow of a tree. You can't see shadow water from a distance. You can't tell how deep it is. You never know what is in it (maybe an alligator, or a snapping turtle as big as a house). But join in the shadow and you can see deep, to the rocks. For June this represents False River, the oxbow lake northwest of Baton Rouge where the Mississippi River has taken another course, and left a C-shaped lake behind. June remembers his grandfather taking him to put meat in barrels in False River, in the clean flowing water, to be stored and cured. It was work usually done by the women, but June's grandfather showed him how to put the meat on a wire grill and close the barrel and put it in a hole dug in the bank. The barrel had nail holes all around so the water could flow through. After a few days they went to retrieve the meat and it was smaller, more pure. The fat and skin were left on the bottom of the barrel. "That was some smart," June says.

I imagine that lakeside visit occurred early in the morning. In the song the refrain "early that morning/early in the morning" is sung in chorus over and over, with increasing tempo as the braves compete.

"You and me!"
"Early in the morning."
"Don't make me beg!"
"Early in the morning."
"Don't make be beg!"
"Early in the morning."
"Don't make me fall."
"Early that morning."
"I'll take him down."
"Early in the morning."

And the leader joins everyone in singing "earleeeeeey, early in the morning."

"They're trying to figure out which one to pick, to go get him, and there's a party going on. It might not ever happen, but they're saying they're not going to be pushed around," says June.

Another brave makes his case:

"I got my Queen."
"Early that morning."
"She know the way."
"Early in the morning."
"I'll make him kneel."
"Early in the morning."
"I'll make him pray!"
"Early in the morning."
"I'm going down!"
"Early that morning."
"Yes I'm going down!"
"Early in the morning."
"I seen his shadow."
"Early in the morning."
"He big and tall!"
"Early in the morning."

Soon another brave steps up amid the drums and the chorus, amid lots of bragging and chanting ("On Mardi Gras morning, they know I don't play, hey!"), his words coming too fast for the people to get a word in edgewise:

"I'll make him scream!
I'll make him shout!
He big and tall!
I make him fall!
I seen his shadow.
Be not afraid.
I'll make him walk

On shadow water.
You and me!
Don't make me beg!"

The song builds and grows like a tide, to become a running, rhythmic, blast of energy, and the people join in strong, continuing to sing between the lines as the braves sing:

"We da Renega- yades!
We da Renega- yades!
Down in New Orleans, y'all!
Say nobody hoom- bow!
On Mardi Gras mor- ning
Say we don't know how, y'all.
My knees start to sweatin', law!
We jump in 'e water!
My baby daugh- ter
Say, 'Take 'em down, June, yo!'
Say nobody hoom- bow!
Say nobody run- now!
We'll knock 'em down, y'all!"

All that before the Wild Man steps up to sing. And the early morning theme continues. "Renegade People" begins: "Mardi Gras morning, we gon' run." And in "Take Your Chances," his dad's favorite, June sings:

"Came home early one morning, had trouble on her mind.
Just couldn't take her heavy load.
Seem like she was wasting her time.
Always complaining.

Seems like everything is wrong.
Say she didn't want me, anymore.
Come on baby, take your chances."

The last song on The Bayou Renegades' deep and unusual self-titled CD, "The Real Deal," is a funky groove and street symphony with the refrain, "won't somebody, treat me right." June flies away on his guitar. Geechie provides new beats with the old Indian walking instruments: bass drum, cowbell. Nunez holds steady on the bass guitar, maybe tired of buying new strings. There are breaks in the action when June seems to sample a few notes of the introduction to The Eagles' "Hotel California"—just an outline—then he is off at running speed playing a hundred notes for every one sampled. And the chorus sings, "Won't somebody, treat me right? What goes on in the dark, uh comes back in the light."

The morning theme reflects June's habits in life.

"Because I don't sleep, they called me the 'Night Tripper' overseas," he says. "I'm always up early in the morning to see the sun rise. That's something spiritual."

He remembers that sometimes on the road, when sunrise came, he'd make them pull the bus over and he'd get out and walk, to greet the coming day.

"A wolf hollers at the moon," says June. "I'm on another level. That's the most precious time of the day: early in the morning. The rooster crows in the morning. There's something about that."

Party for Peace

Reflecting his culture as he did with his music, June, the renegade Indian guitar player who tried to be loyal to the tradition and the people, rather than one tribe or another, became a friend to many tribes in the New Orleans Indian community. People connect through music. It brings us together. June has used music to bring Indian tribes together in his efforts to spread peace in the community.

He recalls organizing a St. Joseph's Night party at Charlie B's "by the convention center" of a big crowd of Indians in the early 1990s, attended by celebrity musician Quincy Jones and Marc Morial, who was running for mayor of New Orleans. It might have been the biggest St. Joseph's Night gathering of New Orleans Indians in history, with Indians from all over town, but without enough light, without enough space for the Indians in suits. At first they were going to award the best-dressed Indian, but decided to give every Big Chief a trophy instead. It was an opportunity to celebrate shared culture, to party and get loaded. They "had so many Indians and so many people coming, they had to block the street," June recalls. "The police, I heard him taking on the radio, 'There's five hundred more Indians over here!' " The Indians came with guns and knives, many of which were taken at the door.

"They had the whole place surrounded. When they let you in, they have to search you. The cops called me in the back. They had a room, and when he opened the door, he said, 'Look at this!' Guns! Knives! Stacked up this high! He said, 'Every m- f- coming in here, June, got a weapon!' Ha ha.

"They had a room full, and then these guys was coming in after, say, 'June, this knife that I had came from my old grandfather that was a Indian, I've gotta get it back.' So people like that, I got them their weapons back. But guns? You couldn't get that back."

There were growing numbers of NOPD officers. June thought they were about to shut the gathering down. At one point candidate Morial stepped to the microphone and used the opportunity to deliver a stump speech to the crowd of Indians, so "nobody could take care of their business," says June.

"They got the biggest crowd you ever want to see, and that's all he needed to tell them what he wanted to do," says June of Morial, who won the election. "So all the police around, they had to bow down. If you're going to break up the event, you got trouble."

As for the Indians, "They could have caused trouble along the way. But when they got in my arena, everybody was so high, at one point, they was just layin' all over. It was a big arena. My daddy said, 'It's a d- shame.' They was so f- up. They couldn't fight, they couldn't do nothing."

He feels like things could have gone badly, without the right people, at the right place, at the right time.

"I always helped people, even if they didn't like me," says June. "I didn't want to see it burned down."

There is a deep respect for Native American cultures here among the Indians of New Orleans. June admires the Chiricahua Apache, Cochise, for his strategy and his focus on the Stronghold, and the people. The first verse of "Down On the Bayou" was inspired by a movie about Cochise and the Apache Wars, Broken Arrow, which June saw as a child, then later reset in song, shifting the scene to his homeland of south Louisiana and bringing along the heroes of his own culture—Spyboy, Big Chief.

June used his connections to arrange a show at Tipitina's featuring Big Chiefs who had serious differences resulting in ugliness, threatening to get worse. June asked Big Chief Lionel Delpit from Downtown, Big Chief Rody Lewis from Uptown (June's cousin), and Uptown Wild Man Ivory Holmes (June called him Big Ivory) to get together for the show, and the people loved it.

"I promoted Lionel, but Rody and Big Ivory, they liked to be around me because I could do that Indian and play the guitar," says June. Though they were from different parts of town and different tribes, of Big Chief Lionel he says, "I got to liking him so much. So I throws a concert at Tipitina's and I hired him to sing (June's song 'Downtown'), and that's when we got to be friends."

All these Big Chiefs are now deceased. Together that night, they sang June's song, which has only seen limited release but is usually heard at June's live shows. The Indians improvised around the catchy—but tricky—line, "If you don't wanna fight, take your black ass downtown." June describes Big Chief Lionel as "so bad," when he took the mic.

"He just got straight to the point. That was a bad piece of lyrics. You'll never hear another piece like that."

And there was Indian music when there might have been more bloodshed, in New Orleans.

In January 2020, June was preparing to release 'Downtown' on a collaborative CD with Chief Kenny Young and Big Chief Howard Miller of the Creole Wild West.

'He Loves Indian Music'

Spy got 'em runnin', got 'em in sight
Pretty White Eagle, dressed in white.
Yellow Pocahontas, the Tchoupitoulas, too.
Uptown ruler, they know what to do.
Creole Wild West, I say Creole Wild West,
Wild Magnolia, I say Wild Magnolia,
Boy you pretty, I say boy, you pretty.

-June Victory and the Bayou Renegades, 'Hold 'em Joe'

Chief Kenny Young, forty-nine in 2019, has always been an Indian. He stresses he is not a Mardi Gras Indian, as some New Orleans Indians describe themselves, but instead he traces his ancestry back to Native American tribes on the north shore of Lake Pontchartrain. His people have been in south Louisiana for six hundred years. They were shipbuilders up around the Rigolets, where Lake Pontchartrain flows into Lake Borgne and thence into the Gulf of Mexico. One of Young's great uncles fought against the British in the Battle of New Orleans.

Young heads the Black Seminole Indian tribe of New Orleans, and was preparing for a press conference regarding the Black Seminole Tribe of Oklahoma when I reached him by telephone.

"History did not tell our story," says Young. "Some

people think all black people came from Africa. That is not the case."

"To know who you are is a big difference," he says.

Born in Charity Hospital at Tulane Avenue and LaSalle Street, New Orleans, and graduated from Marion Abramson High School in the neighborhood of New Orleans East, Young dresses in his regalia to honor his elders' and ancestors' legacies. He was beading his suit in preparation for Carnival—six months away when we spoke via telephone. I asked about his fingers.

"They feel great," he said. "I live it. I can stick it with the needle all day and still live it. I feel great. June ain't the only one that's crazy.

"You can't survive the concrete jungle if you are not a little bit crazy," he muses.

He has known June about nineteen years. They were introduced by Ernie Vincent, when Young was trying to get an album produced. Young is a singer and a drummer, who started out playing buckets in the French Quarter. There are still kids doing that to this day. I worry about those kids and wonder about the temptations they face. Young considers playing the buckets a constructive pastime.

"It's better to be playing buckets on Bourbon Street than to be somewhere else, selling drugs, getting into trouble," he says, though he admits "it's dangerous sometimes."

But there are people who have harder lives than the kids playing buckets on Bourbon Street.

"It's an honest way to make a dollar," he says.

"I did it for the love of playing drums," he says. "I didn't do it for the hustle."

I watched Young perform when June sat in with

Young's Indian funk band at Checkpoint Charlie's on the edge of the French Quarter in 2017. The band is Fiyawata. June was so excited about Fiyawata he seemed about to burst when he called to tell me about the show. "Dis de real deal, bruh," he said. I was impressed with Young's singing, his seemingly endless catalog of songs, his enthusiastic pounding of the tambourine, and his Indian friends. Now he and June are ready to take Fiyawata and run with it.

"I think we have similar lives, and similar passings," says Young of himself and June. "He loves Indian music. I think there's not a lot of people that love it more than I do. He's one of them.

"It's that feeling," Young says with emotion. "We want to give it to the world. It's the old and the new. When we're together, we're like a mixed drink—we're that Fiyawata."

Funky 544

I took notes and recorded interviews from 2016 through 2019, as I came to know June and his family and friends in New Orleans. I was living in New Orleans but working full time in Tennessee—driving back for a pile of assignments and writing them out in New Orleans over a few weeks. And often staring at the south Louisiana sky. You rarely see any big water from Uptown, but you can see its reflection in the blue sky. You can see the big water sending in clouds in wisps or sideways rain. I spent my time worrying about storms, walking my dogs, working on my dad, Frank Andrews', second book, and writing in the back of a yellow shotgun house on Tchoupitoulas Street at a desk jammed in beside the washing-machine. The washer sometimes jumped around and made as much noise as a big rig on the uneven floor.

Among the friends of June's that I interviewed were members of the band working the weekend afternoon shift at the Funky 544 on Bourbon Street, where June went to sit in with and then substitute for Ernie Vincent. Playing as The Mojo Shakers were a blues singer and harmonica player named Mark Appleford; a drummer named Brad "Lefty" Keith; a bass player who rode a Harley Davidson, and was somewhat of a mystery to me; the blues singer Tommy Singleton, in whom Ernie has so much interest; and Ernie Vincent, the featured artist. Everybody was in another band and had a lot of other things going on. The Funky 544 afternoon show is not a showcase for the original work of these talented musicians, but instead seeks to hold onto a light-drinking trickle of customers who happen in off Bourbon Street with hits they recognize after just a few notes. They sometimes group up in a bunch drinking and listening to music, and sometimes turn right around and leave. Playing for them is a job for these musicians and it pays well, compared to some other places around town. It pays enough for June to tip me as his driver.

I interview Appleford. He is tall and lean, clean cut but with a lot of beard stubble, dressed in a plaid shirt rolled up at the sleeves and blue jeans. His hair is a light brown, his eyebrows prominent, his brown eyes friendly and honest. Like me, he prefers daylight hours in New Orleans. He has been robbed twice on the way home from gigs. People see an instrument—they know you are taking home cash. Some people are lowlife enough to take what you have earned by the sweat of your brow and the callouses you are building on your lips blowing harmonica. One good thing about the harmonica: It hides in a man's pocket. It is not so obvious that he is walking home, or to his car, from a gig. Perhaps the highlight of the Funky 544 set is Appleford's soulful but ironic rendition of "I Got A Woman" by Ray Charles. Appleford occasionally substitutes "over on the West Bank" for "way over town" and people love it. His latest CD is called *Voodoo.* It is desperate, crying blues.

I interview Lefty. He loves to play drums. He has silver hair on the sides, and wears a T-shirt and blue jeans. He is about middle height; and not much heavier than he needs to be, to keep walking. He has a lot of things going on. I buy a copy of his 2015 CD, *Lefty Keith*

& The True Blues Vol. 2. Featuring at least fifteen musicians, it showcases Lefty and his friends covering legends, songs recorded in three states. There are songs by musicians I've heard of—B.B. King and T. Bone Walker, Robert Johnson—and some I have not heard of but should have: Roland Stone, L.B. Scott.

This gig at Funky 544—three hours on, hour-and-a-half break, then three more hours playing the hits—seems brutal to me but it is easy for Lefty: easy, and a good job. The only thing is, there is too much noise at the back of the tiny stage. Sandwiched as he is between a brick wall with a window onto Toulouse Street at his back, and a high plastic shield protecting the band from his drum beats at his front, Lefty can see but cannot hear a thing and has to wing it. He watches the other musicians, especially the bassist, for cues. The music crashes around back there like laundry in the wash, making no sense. He nonetheless keeps the beat by eyeball and instinct, and leads the band sometimes, interacting with whatever crowd there is from behind the drum kit, so those out front can take a break. Out in the club you can hear Lefty's deep voice saying this and saying that but you can only catch a stray word due to the sound system or acoustics. Funky 544 is for drinking and partying, with music for support. These guys shine anyway, playing for a big crowd or a few people or nobody, in the hopes that people will hear them and step into the cool, dim room, buy a drink and leave a tip.

June is here at Ernie Vincent's request. He sits in, studies the music, and comes back as lead and rhythm guitar, sharing singing duties with Appleford and Singleton while Vincent is out of town. June and the guys play greatest hits such as "(Sittin' On) The Dock of the Bay," "Stand By Me," "Lowrider," "House of the Rising Sun," and "Mustang Sally": on and on and on. June finds places to rip and slide and send notes dancing around the bar. I play music fan sometimes, whooping and cheering. When Vera is here she is an elastic and light-stepping dancer, the band calls out to her, strangers cheer her from the back of the club. She dresses for the dance floor, not in her Indian suit. She is the queen of the dance floor in her silver pants and flashy shoes and burgundy hair. She steps and sways and moves around the room. She teaches me how to walk the dog.

Sometimes it is too loud and I go outside. I roll cigarettes and watch the people walking by on Bourbon Street. Everybody comes here at one time or another. I get surrounded by a small group of tough-looking men: Obviously not tourists, they are attracted by the cigarette rolling and get in very close to ask questions. The Funky 544 doorman comes to my rescue, gets right in the middle of our little group, and the men disperse. I am grateful. They probably did not mean any harm—but it is good to be looked out for.

I walk around the corner onto Toulouse, and watch the band through the window. I am behind the band here, peering in. I feel sorry for Lefty, crammed back here against the window. June says the drummer is the hardest working member of any band, and that seems especially true in Lefty's case. I am worried about June. He is not a young man. He stands for hours and hours playing these old songs for a trickle of disinterested tourists, often leaning on a stool. He sometimes looks like he is going to pass out, sometimes erupts in attitude and guitar licks, stringing flurries of notes together and making people cheer. He is dressed in white again, over a black Muhammad Ali T-shirt. He wears a silver chain now, and a black fedora, and what appear to be women's sunglasses. They look great on June.

I bring him back and forth from Riverside to the French Quarter to hear his stories, and earn a tip for my work. It is hard to get to a Bourbon Street job: with traffic and street closures and box trucks taking a long time to get around corners. Pedestrians cross without looking to see if you'll stop and once the flow begins you can be stopped for a good long time waiting for others to cross. Bicycles fly through silently, sirens blare, rideshares stop, pedicabs snake through ringing their bells, somewhere people cheer for something and the music flows out of the clubs night and day. It is hard to find parking, and the nearest curbside spot might be blocks away. I drive right up to Funky 544, sometimes on Bourbon, sometimes on Toulouse, where I block part of the street while we unload June's guitar in the coffin case, and his heavy amp into the club. They think I am with the band, and I never have to pay.

On a busy Sunday evening I am parked illegally at Bourbon and St. Louis, facing the lake, beside Big Easy Daiquiris. We are down here to collect June's money. Bourbon Street is closed to cars, and packed with pedestrians. June springs out of the car and goes into the flood of people, looking this way and that. Lefty shows up, waiting for his money, too. Mark Appleford arrives. They gather beside Fat Catz on the riverside/uptown corner, across St. Louis Street from Chris Owens'. I watch from outside my car. I am watching for anybody with a ticket book or worse, a tire boot, but also watching the street and the people. I am keeping a lookout for the daiquiri-shop girl who will come out and slap you hard on the rear end. I always keep an eye out for people I might know from Tennessee. There is a beautiful rosy glow as club lights enhance the waning daylight.

It seems like we are waiting a long time and June is back and forth, checking on me, checking with Appleford and Lefty. He looks up and down Bourbon Street. There are people of every description heading downtown, heading uptown, having the time of their lives, or looking for customers or victims. I marvel at the trouble to which a musician has to go, getting down here and collecting money in this sea of people. There is a terrible stench in the air at this time. The city will later discover some restaurants have been emptying their grease traps into the storm sewers, and clean out the backed-up storm sewers, but they have not discovered it yet and now and then a strong sewer smell envelops us as we wait, then blows away on the slight breeze to be replaced by a delicious seafood smell.

"I hate this street!" June says grumpily.

Soon the bass player shows up on his motorcycle, parks right in the street, and pays the band. I make my way inch-by-inch out of the French Quarter then head uptown through the Central Business District by way of Basin and Loyola. Wrung out and looking very green, slumped into the passenger's seat, June gives patient, quiet directions on the twenty-minute crosstown drive. We pass beneath the Pontchartrain Expressway, through Central City and into Broadmoor, and take Napoleon almost to the river. We are both glad to be back in our uncrowded, quiet neighborhood.

'He's Dangerous'

Hey, Mardi Gras
Chief's been drinking that fire water!

-June Victory and the Bayou Renegades, 'Mardi Gras Time'

We are bumping along a potholed Uptown street, and June has just a minute to talk. He has stories for a long ride, or a short one. This is a short ride. "Mary Ann McGrath Swaim is a billionaire, and she's my friend," he says. "They were talking to her one time, some mens. And she said, 'Oh yeah, June is a good guy, he's very disciplined, but he's dangerous,' yeah. Ha ha ha!"

A Good Catch

Zulu is rolling! We have made it from Riverside to Ms. Sadie's in Central City and the great parade is moving riverbound under the Jackson Avenue trees. The sidewalk is packed, and I am here with my wife Ginny and our thirteen-year-old daughter Violet in front of the salon, and we are all glad to be a part of this tradition. Ms. Sadie makes sure we are all right and June looks out for us. Vera is so excited about the parade. Me, too. I wouldn't trade this, my sidewalk spot by Ms. Sadie's, for any other spot in the city.

Zulu rolls early and comes here first; it was a struggle to cross town, park, and walk the several blocks to the salon, but it is more than worth it as the riders are happy to be starting and the throws are tremendous. The crowd cheers and everyone raises their arms to the passing floats, hollering and smiling for a trinket or a prize. People on the sidewalk look for people they know behind the masks, and normally introverted and quiet people like Ginny emerge from their shells and freak out for plastic beads. I am absorbed in the scene, catching something here and there, watching the floats, watching the happy people, trying to keep up with June who darts here and there saying hello. I want to see the Zulu King. Vera hands me a coconut. "For Ginny," she says. Someone throws a full bag of beads my way but I don't notice. It is about the size of a softball, softer but heavier, heading straight for Violet's face. I see it but not in time to react. It is a shadow in the corner of my eye getting larger about to hit her face when I look up.

In an instant a hand reaches out and long bony fingers close around the bag, *thwack*! June catches the bag of beads two feet from Violet's face and saves Mardi Gras Day. I'll never forget him for that.

'This Town's Crazy'

Mardi Gras season brings traffic snarls around New Orleans. Someone who studies the newspaper could avoid the parades but I never seemed to be able to keep up and frequently found myself stuck in traffic. I also try to avoid elevated highways, which we do not have many of in Tennessee, but are often the only way to get anywhere around New Orleans.

I drive Tchoupitoulas most of the way downtown. I should drive lakebound from the river on Napoleon Avenue, take a right on South Claiborne Avenue and be catapulted onto a bridge for about a fifteen minute ride to the French Quarter. But I prefer Tchoupitoulas which hugs the firm ground of the riverbank and could take the same amount of time, or much longer depending on parades, anything happening at Walmart, the Mercedez Benz Superdome or the Warehouse District art galleries, or any number of things. Plus Tchoupitoulas plays out, becoming one way uptown before you get to Poydras Street, and you have to go around and use South Peters Street to get to Canal Street.

June and I get caught in gridlocked traffic near Canal Street with both downtown-bound lanes of South Peters backed up for a block, pedestrians crossing between cars, cars pushing to change lanes.

"Look at this! This town's crazy," says June as we stop and go, stop and go in the canyon of buildings, every driver staying at least four inches from the motorist beside and in front of him.

Near Canal Street we see what has clogged traffic: A police officer has blocked Canal Street lakebound as well as access from South Peters Street to North Peters Street and the French Quarter. That is my way into the French Quarter: barricaded for some reason. So we turn right on Canal with a lot of other people, circle back around because there is nowhere to go that direction except the river. The situation has stopped traffic going into the Quarter and getting away from the Quarter so a lot of cars are circling and people are sounding their horns. June is in a hurry to get to a show an hour early, the required arrival time. "Pull up here," he tells me as we near the barricade.

One cannot get anything done sitting in the car in a situation like this—I guess. June exits, walks from the car to the policeman and talks briefly. It is easy to believe he is a guitar player trying to get to the show. Dressed in white, with a jaunty hat and dancing braids, he gestures and smiles at the policeman, and he sounds like he's singing just talking—he has this deep gravelly voice. Pretty soon the policeman walks over to the barricade and helpfully swings it out of the way as June hurries to the car.

"Now we won't have to go all the way around, so that's good," says June as I drive into the French Quarter via Decatur and St. Louis.

June later has a chance to discuss New Orleans philosophically, as someone who is attached to this place and part of its character like the southern live oak trees in Audubon Park. We take a break there from the dense city, sitting on a bench under the Tree of Life, as wary hyenas eye Audubon Zoo groundskeepers working in the enclosure at our backs.

"I love New Orleans," June tells me. "I may not agree with the way they run the system. It's very confusing. And you're going to have people come in with all different ideas, when it come how to run this town or what it need or what it don't need. But if you would walk in the French Quarter right now, you'll find kids tap dancing, you'll find some of them playing buckets, you'll find some guy telling a story—he's homeless with no shoes. You'll find people walking around trying to sell beads. You'll find all this stuff. They don't deprive them of making a living.

"Not only that, the people here is so loose on helping each other. You can meet people, and if you just move next door to someone, they'll knock on your door and say welcome to the neighborhood. And they're really serious about it. If you're in a jam or in trouble, they'll come to your aid, to help you. It's like everyone that live in New Orleans is kin to one another. That's how they do it. It's like family. And as soon as you meet somebody they want to know what's your name, and what part of the city you come from, or who you know. And eventually by talking to them you're going to find some way that you fit into the agenda. That's something."

The Return of Cabbage Alley

Earl Johnson, seventy-five and a resident of New Orleans East in 2019, was born and raised in Uptown New Orleans and has known June since the mid-1950s. Johnson ran with the Indians, but not in a role. His tribe is the Wild Magnolias, and he just likes walking with the people.

"I just wanted to be an Indian, that's all, just get out and mask," he says in a telephone interview.

He has been married over twenty years to Trina Johnson, a Big Queen of the Golden Eagles Mardi Gras Indians.

Johnson is part of June's vision for a new Cabbage Alley and he remembers it very well.

"Aw, man, it was a beautiful place on the corner of Philip and Danneel," says Johnson. "They had a shoe shop, they had houses around, people be sitting out. On the corner was the neighborhood bar, you know, where we used to go on Friday, Saturday, Sunday.

"It was a dead-end street. They had another alley they used to call Carnage Alley at the end of Saratoga—they were in there dealing drugs."

Carnage Alley was also called Pork Chop Alley. Carnage Alley/Pork Chop Alley adjoined Cabbage Alley so it was easy to go out of one and into the other.

Johnson says, "People used to sit out every day and nobody bothered anybody. Oh, man, it was a hangout for everybody. Everybody used to come from all around just to hear each other play, bands and singers coming from all over.

"The audience was beautiful, no trouble whatsoever. No (need for) police or anything. They just sat down and looked at them playing. They had some would get up and dance. We'd sit around, do a little smoking, whatever."

Johnson helped with traffic—making sure cars stayed away from people.

"They had people standing on the sidewalks, standing on the street," he says.

Other than that, Cabbage Alley didn't need much security. "Everybody was security," says Johnson. What security there was did not need weapons. "None whatsoever," he says.

"Nobody had no weapons then. Everybody was getting along just fine," he says. "Everybody was having a good time, a fun time."

In addition to the Bayou Band and visiting musicians, Johnson recalls the stage featuring New Orleans Indians in casual dress singing "Ooh Na Nay" and "Wild Magnolia."

"Everybody would clean up after," says Johnson.

"Everybody would pick up paper" and get ready for the next week. They'd be gone by around 10 p.m. as most had to work Monday morning.

He likes June's plan to bring the music back to Cabbage Alley.

"Yes, sir ree, do it again," says Johnson. "The stage and stuff is still right there."

While he is bringing live music back to Cabbage Alley, June wants to bring Earl Johnson along, too, and the other elders who are still around, as honorary security.

"Cabbage Alley was a big event," says June. "The return of Cabbage Alley is a spiritual thing."

Earl Nunez

Earl Nunez was fifty-eight in November 2019. June says Earl's bass line "opened the gates for me." He recruited Earl when Earl was still a teenager, twelve years his junior, for his funky bass line.

"His momma was kind of nervous, but she knew I would take care of him," June says.

Says Earl, "A friend of mine introduced me to June. He brought June to my house."

He doesn't remember his mother being worried. "Mom, she was the type of person, she ain't gonna tell me, she's gonna tell him, if she's worried about me going out."

Earl is quiet, youthful, and meticulous. He often seems lost in thought; he has a strong under-bite, which makes him seem to be looking upward. He has good luck. We make a U-turn on Tchoupitoulas Street aiming for downtown and June's pouch, left on the roof, blows off the car and catches the wind and flies through the cracked window right into Earl's hands.

We are very busy when I meet Earl. June is suddenly swamped with requests to play. His life is different than it was when I met him in 2016, when it seems he was mostly sitting in the park. While I used to have June to myself for hours, I now have to join in his entourage somehow—this weekend, as driver—and we strategize about his book in stops and starts.

Before heading downtown we are loading gear into the car and Earl is tuning a new five-string bass guitar: a gleaming rust-and-white, twenty-three-hundred-dollar Music Man, that after playing live he says is "worth every penny." He plays five-string bass for a deeper bottom, and a better range. When he is not fine-tuning the bass, which is ringing perfectly on the electronic chart, he is going back and forth to his truck. Earl is a mechanic in Lafayette and his Chevy Tahoe shines and is loaded with highlights. He walks past me to the truck and starts opening and closing the driver's-side door, looking at the hinges, opening and closing. I don't hear a thing. He finds and applies WD-40. He still seems unsatisfied. But he closes the door and goes around and checks the passenger's side too, opening and closing the door.

Earl cannot stand June's smoking but he is staying with June for the weekend and so is unable to escape it. He complains a lot about June's cigarettes, saying he is choking and going to a different room in the house, or keeping his window down in the car (luckily). He shows his annoyance and aggravation over the smoke but in rehearsal, never argues with June despite June's high-tempered directions and lectures.

He plays a bass line that brought that instrument to life for me, because I never knew it could be played like a drum. Before I met Earl I had been listening to Renegades music almost constantly for about six months and walking everywhere to Earl's bass line—*thumpa de dump dump, da dump, da, thumpa de dump dump da dump, da*—and every now and then he pops off a note so you think he broke a string. And it's that note that turns walking into jumping making it fun. It's that note that takes this out of the ordinary. It's that note that the tricksters wanted gone, because it can't be machinated.

Nobody taught Earl to do that. He calls it his trademark.

He was supposed to play trumpet. He did play trumpet, as a child. But he dreamed of playing bass. He wanted to play with the drummers, but on bass guitar. He was closest to his mother, but has a fond memory of the day when his dad said, "Come on, Earl, let's go someplace.

"He told me to come get in the truck, and come with him," says Earl.

Earl's dad didn't say where they were going. Earl remembers pulling up in front of the music store at North Broad Avenue and Bayou Road. The father spent a minute or two trying to talk the son into playing lead guitar, but that is not what the boy wanted. He wanted that bass: a four-string is what they had in those days. He went home with a cheap Fender copy and was ready to play with the drummers. He was fourteen years old. Pretty soon he replaced the knock-off with a professional guitar that cost fifteen hundred dollars.

He recalls fondly his days of touring with June and Monk Boudreaux and Bo Dollis of the Wild Magnolias.

"I would get a newspaper the next day when we was leaving, and a lot of the talk was about me and June," says Earl. "They called me 'Thunder and Lightning.' We way out here in Vermont, over in France, Japan, and they're talking about me and June, how we sounded."

Jasmin Cardriche

Recruited by June to replace Dog and still playing drums decades later, Jasmin lives a highly regulated life being available on a moments' notice to drive workers for the oil industry. If she is spending any time with the band she has to take the whole day off because she cannot be in the session and miss the call to get her passengers. She is serious about drumming and driving and you have to be. The drum kit takes up most of a fifteen-passenger van, not to mention amps and mics and cords; and the workers must run on schedule to meet the helicopters going offshore with no room for being late. Both jobs are all about timing.

Jasmin is a hard worker, strong like drummers have to be, and dressed for cold weather when I meet her in a practice space somewhere in New Orleans: a heatless bay in a self-storage garage much weathered and decaying outside and inside, too cold for me to sit down. Under carpeted walls and spidery ceiling the Bayou Renegades practice music that touches me to the core, that I have been listening to on repeat for months, and I can't believe I am here. Vera is here, and Tommy Singleton, and Earl and June. While the band is playing Tommy hands me a cowbell and a drum stick, and that is my chance—to play with The Bayou Renegades!—and I blow it: shyly nodding no, but thanking Tommy later for the opportunity. I did not know where to put the cowbell in the song.

Jasmin is bundled up in thick clothes and beanie behind her drum kit, watching June intently all the time. She seems to play only for June: not worrying much about Earl who is too good to need much worrying about. Jasmin watches June's fingers like a sports fan watches a close football game on TV, eyes wide, trying to see every movement. She seldom needs to look at her drums: just June.

The next day on Frenchmen Street I watch Jasmine load into a club for a sound check and it seems like backbreaking labor. I am lucky to be June's driver instead of his drummer. She parks by a flooded gutter—with very dirty water, since the weather has been dry a few days—and reaches into the van bringing out cases and cases of drums, carrying them over the dirty water and down a long hall to the stage. Someone comes up and parks behind the van leaving barely enough room. Jasmin just keeps unloading, squeezing into whatever space is left, working, working. Then it's more work onstage setting everything up and not much sound checking needed for the drummer. So she sits and smiles, ready to provide the beats when they are needed.

I catch her outside on the sidewalk. She is walking the sidewalk looking for a place selling food. I think Earl has had something to do with her being out here, because he was worrying all the way over here about a Burger King, and we never passed one. Now there is not much open on Frenchmen Street even though it seems like it should be lunchtime. I walk beside Jasmin lakebound a block or so where we find a pizza and chicken place, but all they have right now is chicken, and Jasmin wants pizza or a hamburger or something.

Finding nothing else open we make our way back to the club, where Jasmin has to go in and deliver the bad news. While I am still outside June comes out looking around, also looking for something to feed the band. Somehow a man comes along with a box of bananas. June negotiates with the man for a bunch of bananas and runs in to feed Earl and Jasmin bananas.

***

That night I get to introduce The Bayou Renegades to the crowd: a sizable crowd in a dark theater. It is the day after Halloween and decorative spider webs still cover the chandeliers. There is room for dancing in front of the band and several round tables for ten or so people arranged around. June's family and friends make a whole table up front. Ernie Vincent is sitting in with the Renegades: June and Earl and Jasmin. Also sitting in is Hubie Vigreux, a lifelong musician and percussionist who remembers coming to this club when it was a printing plant and picking up his first business cards.

"Born in the Ninth Ward, back in the Ninth Ward," Vigreux tells me before the show.

Also on hand is Tommy Singleton, to offer some heartbreaking blues. Chief Kenny Young is here with drumsticks across his back like arrows, singing Indian songs and some of the Renegades songs. He brings a second drummer, also a female, also named Jasmine; she is creative and strong all around.

The band plays "Mardi Gras Time" and "Hold 'em Joe" from The Bayou Renegades' archive, and the Wild Magnolias' "Smoke My Peace Pipe (Smoke It Right)," among other tunes.

The music seems great from the dance floor, though it does not suit June. I get so caught up listening to Earl's bass lines, and dancing with friends I never get to see anymore, that I miss the cue to come up and talk about June's book—which at the time does not exist.

Vera dances around with me and a sprinkling of others who are dancing. June's daughter Yolanda and her daughter are here dancing and Yolanda adds a strong trilling in support of the band. Many people accidentally sat in glue, or something. As the few of us are dancing and June is playing that soaring guitar Vera goes up and points to him and says, "That's my brother! That's my bruhtherrrr!"

Vera leaves and comes back in her Indian suit, a splash of color with two big fans, and moves up to the stage to dance beside June for a long time.

While listening and dancing to "Cherie," I forget that I am supposed to shake the tip bucket around to encourage the crowd during this song, because "somebody's got to pay." A lot of things don't happen that are supposed to happen while June plays for two hours, leading everyone the whole time, until he looks around forcefully at the band members and pulls his finger across his neck, cut. He lays his guitar haphazardly across an amp and staggers behind the curtain.

The band stops immediately and the room goes quiet and it seems like a strange close, to me. Vera and June's daughter rush behind the curtain and stay. I go back there and June is slumped onto the little stairway, drenched in sweat, his hands over his head, with the women close around him worrying.

He says he has had two strokes, but stands up long enough to pack his guitar and gear. I rush for the car and we get him away from Frenchmen Street and back uptown. June thinks he has had strokes because he is wet with sweat, but not cold. He has been through this before. Everyone wants him to go to the hospital but fearing they would keep him he refuses. He goes home and into a near-boiling bath with a towel draped over him, stays in the water as long as he can stand it, then drinks an herbal tea, clears his bowels explosively, and rests.

Vera later tells me the show paid forty-eight dollars, all of it tips.

June doesn't complain. He cancels an appearance at a different club for the following day but is back on stage less than a week later.

Mildred (Guerian) Victorian

Way uptown in New Orleans, South Claiborne Avenue is a frenetic hubub of activity. Three lanes head uptown, toward Tulane University and Carrollton. Three lanes head downtown, toward the Superdome. The speed limit is 35 mph and we all want to use every single one of them, if not more. The middle lane is the best for through traffic. The left lane always gets stopped for people trying to turn left or make a legal U-turn. The right lane stops for people turning and is also likely to play out or be forced to turn. The middle lane goes along at a steady clip and is sometimes used as a passing lane. Just before Toledano Street, headed uptown, is a destination shopping center with stores Ginny and I always seemed to be driving to from far across the city: stores with clothes and makeup and things. There is a busy scene of cars and lights and shops and running down the middle, a beautiful neutral ground recently restored and used regularly by old men who sit and talk, by young people who collect money from stopped cars for their dance troupes or youth groups. Here and there a homeless person begs silently with a ragged sign. This is a scene of a busy corridor in a fast-moving, sometimes confusing city.

Turn right onto Louisiana Avenue Parkway, lakebound. The Parkway begins here, and the scene changes suddenly. Oaks line left and right and their branches tower over. Ahead is a tunnel of green over two traffic lanes, with no traffic. Colorful, stately homes stand behind sidewalks on either side. Here and there a house is divided into doubles or apartments and all the homes face sidewalks in the shade or spots of welcome sun. You think you are on St. Charles Avenue.

This is a street of luminaries and dignitaries, and everybody. It is a mixed street where someone of any race or income could find a place—poor to rich. It is the kind of street cities are spending millions to create—where affordable housing coexists with the homes of the well heeled. Still headed lakebound, driving under the oaks on the solid concrete, you might pass a house with several young men hanging about in a treadworn front yard, a junk car sitting out front. You will pass a jewel of a house with gated lawn and what surely looks like a police car standing outside. You'll pass the homes of current and former mayors of New Orleans, and a former home of the legendary producer Master P.

Almost to South Broad Avenue now, on the right, is Mildred Victorian's house. It stands freshly painted, violet and inviting early this morning on a chilly fall day. There was nine feet of water in this house after Katrina, when Mildred lost everything. It is a full two-story double, stucco with a tile crown and a wide, low palm plant out front, still in the shade when I arrive. Individual sidewalks lead from a hulking oak tree by the street to the two entrances: Mildred's house downstairs, and Vera's house upstairs. Each unit has a screened porch overlooking the yard and the trees. Each sidewalk is accented with a real wagon wheel brought to this place from False River by Vic Victorian after he and Mildred bought the house in 1971, and still standing long after Vic's passing: now set in concrete, as though stuck, and sometimes attracting tourists with questions, which the occupants do not mind, even enjoy.

"I've gotta go by my mom's house," June has said to me so many times and often it has been the beginning of an adventure. Once after a rare period of freezing weather the water stopped running all over town—or else it burst from pipes flooding crawlspaces and sidewalks, and worse. Few people are prepared here for freezing weather. My crawlspace was not skirted by anything—just open to the elements and inside the house, when the sun was right, you could see through cracks in the floor. Waking that morning with no water I thought it must be frozen pipes. Certainly the wood floor was freezing cold. There was not a single plumber that I could find to answer the phone. I brought out extension cords and a hair dryer and crawled that long shotgun from backyard hose bib to the sidewalk connection, on my back, heating the pipe with the hair dryer as I crawled along. Bundled in all my cold-weather clothes, pushing a tarp ahead of me in the cold dirt, I inspected and heated every inch of pipe and never found a frozen spot. The pipes were not frozen. It turned out we were having a pressure problem, along with a lot of other people. When I dragged myself out of there and into the house I saw that June had called eight times.

"Look, I've got an emergency. I've gotta go by my mom's house," he said when I called back.

It turned out there was water leaking out of the back of Mildred's house and had been for hours when June and I arrived midmorning in the still-freezing weather. We rushed around back and looked into the crawlspace toward the gushing water, which you could hear better than you could see. We went around front, and June dug a little in the front yard looking for the shutoff valve where he had seen it many years before. He couldn't believe it was not where it had always been and dug around in the mud with a stick, cussing the missing valve and the cold weather and this whole mess.

And I was clueless and have often wished, but seldom more so than that cold day, that I had learned useful skills like plumbing and carpentry and working with tools but that is just not the case.

Eventually I had to leave June to figure it out, which he was more than capable of doing, in one way or another, and he never needed me for anything after the ride. But I felt bad for not being able to help in any way, and I didn't get a chance to talk to June's mother that day about her strange and incredible son who is a legend around New Orleans and wrote some of the best rock 'n' roll ever written but is currently without a driver's license—expired, not suspended—or a working car or a house of his own. All he seems to value is his music collection, his guitars and amps and a programmable footboard he is always playing with that sometimes plays a few licks by itself ("It's like it's playing me, back to me, you hear me, bruh?"). When that happens onstage June seems surprised and delighted, and careful listeners in the audience hear it, too, and smiles break out. He could use these guitars and amps and footboard with a life of its own to pick up a few dollars any night of the week. But he is not much interested in gathering dollars except to give them away and collects almost nothing for himself, except music and friends.

When I return to Mildred's house on the Parkway in October 2019, the woman who, with Vic, raised this fantastic character greets me at the door early in the morning, polite and confident beside Vera who is here to help, as she has always been. We walk through the screened porch and living room to the well-appointed dining room, where we sit at the big wooden table in comfortable chairs and after a couple of minutes of greetings Mildred begins to reminisce. She has recently celebrated her ninety-fourth birthday.

"I was born in New Roads, Louisiana, August 27, 1925," she says. "At home. We were all born at home. My momma had us all at the house."

A midwife helped with the birth. Her parents, Augustine and Idell Guerian, farmed cotton and onions and picked pecans and had eleven children, all told. Mildred was the last child, and was the last still living in 2019.

Her parents spoke French. Her mother looked Indian; her father was a light-skinned black man, not as light as Mildred, who June considers white. In fact Mildred's whiteness has been a defining part of June's character: the reason he had to fight both whites and blacks as a child. Mildred's light skin could get her into places darker people could not go, in the bad old days; her children and Vic sometimes waited in the car while she went into such a place. It made June an ally and friend of both whites and blacks (or a hard enemy of either one, trying to do him wrong). He never saw skin color in musicians and thinks it would be self-defeating to decline to work with someone based on color, since what you are looking for is sound.

In this city where colors are so strong it is curious that they can also lose some of their meaning. Mildred and June and I are all somewhere in between black and white.

I ask Mildred if she still speaks French.

"*Parlez Francaise*," she says with a laugh. "That's all

my momma could speak. My daddy, they used to talk to each other, and sometimes they'd speak English. But if they don't want you to know what they're saying, they used to speak French. But they didn't speak much English."

"I always did speak English," she says, though she knew French, or Creole, too.

In her girlhood she wore croaker sack dresses, handmade. She remembers her mother and aunt sewing flour sack slips and such. She remembers playing with her cousins, many of whom lived in New Roads.

"I'd go to their house, they'd come to my house. We used to play ball and things like that, in the yard. The yard was big, big," she says. "We used to have little toys, different toys. They'd bring their toy, and I'd bring mine, and we'd play with toys."

They might have played with store-bought dolls obtained at Christmas, when live trees were decorated outside the house.

"My daddy would light it up," she says. "And they used to have plums. They would decorate with plums. And the children would throw things, and all the plumbs be falling!" she says with a laugh.

"Yeah, you could eat them!" says Mildred.

She never had to work on the farm.

"Because I was the baby, you see. The other ones worked on the farm, not me. I was always in school."

She remembers baths in big tubs of hauled water, remembers having to use outdoor toilets and all kinds of work going on year-round: women sewing and men chopping and stacking wood for winter heat when they were not farming.

"Then a man used to pass, and be selling ice, and my

momma and them would buy the ice and put it in something and we'd have ice," says Mildred.

"It's funny, now my daddy was related to some of them in New Roads, and the man would come, that man was driving like in a wagon. And the mules was pulling the wagon. That man would come and bring the meat and everything, for my momma. I said, 'My momma say, yeah, we's going pay you.' 'Oh no no no,' he told me. 'No, you don't have to pay me.' He said, 'Because, you know, I kin to your daddy.' I say, 'You kin to my daddy?' It was a white man. He say, 'Yeah, I'm kin to your daddy, your daddy know I kin to him. I give you that. Take it, go way.' So he gone, and I didn't pay, uh-uh.

"My daddy was related to all of them, and they liked him. Oh yeah.

"You take like my grandpa, on my momma's side, and my grandma. They buried right in New Roads town, where all the whites buried. Ain't no blacks buried. Just them two: my grandpa, and my grandma. They buried there."

Wilson, Sr. was about four years older than Mildred. She knew him from school. He was thinly built and strong from farm work, with a prominent brow and dark brown skin.

"He was a good person, my husband. Very good. Even though he was nice looking, he was a good person. You look for the goodness, not the prettiest," she says.

"I came down here (New Orleans) and then he followed, too, to come down here. And he was working and I was in school here, at Booker Washington High School."

She lived with her aunt in the Magnolia Projects during this time. It would have been the early to mid-1940s.

"It was a good place, everybody was nice, everybody was good," she says.

Vic arrived on a motorcycle looking for her, after avoiding questions in his hometown and the war raging abroad. He played a couple of tricks to follow the woman he loved. In False River, he told people he was going into the service.

Says Vera, "He did that to leave out from there, to come down here to find momma. My daddy's sister said when he went to take the test or whatever for the service, he ate a piece of Octagon Soap. That you wash clothes with? And that Octagon Soap make your heart beat—slow. So after they checked him, they say he was no good for the service. So he didn't want to go anyway.

"So he left," Vera continues. "She say he came down here on a motorcycle. I never knew he rode a motorbike. Came down here on a motorcycle. And how he found momma, one of dad's cousins told daddy, say, 'If you come here on a Sunday, you're going to see her passing in front of here, with the guy she's taking with now.' That guy's people had a lot of money. They owned a drug store and everything. So when my momma was coming from church, St. Monica, with the guy, my daddy was waiting by the cousin's. They had to pass in front of her door. So when they was passing daddy seen momma, and that's when daddy told momma, you know, just pick who she wanted, say who she wanted, and he'd be going on. And so momma picked daddy, so the boy kept going. And that's how she wound up with daddy—back with daddy."

Mildred says her parents "didn't care about him at first. They didn't understand, no. But afterwards, they liked him. That's why I chose him: because he was a good person."

Mildred and Vic had a try at farming in False River in Pointe Coupee Parish, on the island across the oxbow lake of the same name, from New Roads. Vera was born on the island.

Vic was familiar with hard work. His parents Toussaint Victorian and Mary Alice Charles were dead by the time he was nine. "So my daddy always did work," Vera says.

As a young man with a wife and daughter Vic farmed cotton and picked pecans and discovered some hard economic realities in False River, as Vera recalls.

"I remember he used to get credit at the store for food, whatever we wanted to eat for the year," she says. "And then when the year was up and he'd go to get paid for all the cropping that he done did, they tell him the grocery amount that he owe, that takes care for the year so he gets nothing.

"It was even, and the difference—you don't know. My daddy didn't know. Now my daddy was a brilliant person, for knowing how to survive, and how to, you know, live, but schooling—he had none. He had no schooling. Momma had schooling; my daddy had none. He might have went to second grade, third the most. But you couldn't beat him counting money. He knew how to count money."

Vic and Mildred's first house in New Orleans was on Galvez Street, right off of Third Street. They looked forward to a future of work and both looked downtown for jobs.

Mildred managed the front of the house at Roma Restaurant across Decatur Street from Cafe du Monde, and beside Jackson Square. She did so for fourteen or so years, while the husband-and-wife owners cooked the food.

"I was the boss over that. I was the manager," says Mildred. "They put me to run the place. I was so smart with the money, to check out people, when they order something. And I could collect the money."

She remembers a safe French Quarter. "It was good at that time. Nobody worried you. I used to work there by myself at night, down there all night by myself. Nobody ever bothered me. All them white people used to come there and eat, and all. They never bothered me. No, indeed. They used to look out for me. I worked there all night, I did. I used to run the place, money and all, and nobody ever bothered me. But now it's too bad out there. But when I was working, it wasn't."

Soon June was born, at Charity Hospital, a birth followed by months of anxiety and sleepless nights for Mildred and Vic.

"He stayed in the hospital about four months," Mildred says. "He was sick. But he made it. Thank God he made it, you know. He made it. We took care of him good. My husband used to go every night, and sit up sometimes all night, to the hospital."

Before long the family was living on Philip Street. June was growing into a curious child, and the children stayed with the grandmother next door, who was their babysitter, just watching Vera and June. They called the babysitter Dear. June played his first original tunes on a milk crate in Dear's yard.

Vic worked for Woolworths on Canal Street as a bricklayer. He later worked at the Kaiser Aluminum plant, and for Quaid Fence. Then he went into business for himself doing landscaping, hauling, taking kids to school. He could do a little bit of everything, it sounds like.

Says Mildred, "All them big white people, they all was crazy behind him. They still do. And he's dead now how many years, and they're still crazy about him."

During this period, says Vera, "We barely seen him. He used to work day and night, in a sense. He used to work at night, and when he'd go to work at night, we'd be asleep. And when he'd come back in the morning, we'd be going to school. That happened for a long time, he was working like day and night."

Mildred and Vic used some of their money to send the children to Catholic school.

According to Mildred, "That was the best thing to do at the time: put them in Catholic school. Because the sisters there, the nuns, used to see about them, you know, and teach them the right thing."

Vera says, "In a Catholic school, you was going to learn. They was going to make you learn. At public school, in a sense, they sit there: 'If you want it, you get it. If you don't want it, we got ours.' But in a Catholic school, you're going to learn. Because they would pull your whole ear off. Knock you under here—under your chin. Them nuns was rough, yeah."

Says Mildred, "June was going to ... St. Monica's school on Galvez Street. And he used to be—make like he play music. And the sister called, 'I don't know why he won't try to learn too much. All he wants to do is like play music,' play like guitar, like he play now. They said that's all he know. And the sister said, 'I'm going to tell you something.' She say, 'If he don't want to go graduate, the rest of that, no argue, leave him alone. Because he ain't going to be nothing but a musician.' I said, 'You tink?' She said, 'That's all he's going to be.' She said, 'I'm telling you.' The nun told me this, the sister at St. Monica's, where he was going to school. And that's true. The sister was right. That's all he wanted to be."

At first the Victorians did not want June to be a musician and play in clubs.

"After he decided that he wanted that, my husband and I didn't interfere with that. The sisters told me, 'That's all he's going to be,' " says Mildred.

It was easier for Vic, than Mildred. Vic was on board for whatever his children wanted to do. Mildred admits she did not like Vera running with the Mardi Gras Indians.

"I was afraid something might happen," she says. "I didn't care about that. No. I still don't care about it." She laughs. "I don't care about it at all."

According to Vera, part of that was the dancing in public. But to Vera that seems strange—since Mildred and Vic were dancers too, in their day. Mildred remembers dancing with Vic at Club 49 on False River, "right on the water," where the two were named best dancers.

Vera says they practiced "hand-out dancing, rock 'n' roll, swinging out together."

Later in life Mildred cared for her mother who lived into her eighties.

"She died here in this house," says Mildred. "She died here with me. And I had to take her body back to New Roads to be buried. Where my daddy's buried, that's where she's buried. We took her back.

"So they had the right daughter," says Mildred. "They had a good daughter."

I ask about the time June cut the household telephone cord, to make a microphone.

"June used to do all kinds of things," says Mildred with a long laugh. "I say, 'You go sit down, boy!' June used to do all kinds of funny little tricks. He cut the cord trying to make a microphone, and my husband had to go get another cord."

Vic wasn't angry. "Anything the children do, no, he's not angry. He was a good person," she says.

Victorians in New Orleans

June Victory loves Mardi Gras. His song "Mardi Gras Time" from The Bayou Renegades' Monkey Hill CD is proof enough of that. It mirrors Professor Longhair's "Go To The Mardi Gras," responding to the line "get your ticket in your hand, you want to go to New Orleans" with "got my ticket in my hand, I'm gonna go to New Orleans," and also cheers the town and its legendary party. June's version involves a lot of tambourine and hand drumming: and more rhythm guitar and bass. There is no whistling or piano. It is quieter than one might expect, with an inherent tension. The chorus comes as a shout, maybe a threat: "Hey, Mardi Gras! Chief's been drinking that fire water!" There is recurring shouting in the background—"Flag Boy!" "Big Chief!" "Spyboy!" "Uptown ruler!"—that is hard to understand, until you have seen the Indians parading on Mardi Gras Day. "Mardi Gras Time" was once featured on a Mardi Gras parade throw, before a threatened lawsuit shut that down (not from Professor Longhair, known as Fess, but from June's label).

June loves Mardi Gras so much he has rushed off to Central City wearing a wrong shoe, but we kept going.

Mildred Victorian didn't like Mardi Gras, "not too much," she says. "Well, I would go with them. My husband was going, and we'd go too. But really I didn't care about it too much. Too much crowds. I never used to like to be amongst a crowd. I'm always an inside person. You see like now: Everybody knows that about me around here. They know I don't go nowhere too much."

Says Vera, "But my dad, he would take us to every parade that would come through. I don't know so much if he loveded it, but he was the type of person, whatever we wanted to do, he would back us up. Momma was more of a quiet person, inside person. But my daddy, he wasn't an outside person for the street—let's don't get it twisted—but whatever we wanted to do, or like June wanted to play music, he went all the way.

"He kind of left me to my momma, and he to June," Vera says. "But if it was something I really wanted to do, it was O.K. with him. Momma was on the strict, strict side. But my daddy would go along with us."

Mildred was strict—but gentle.

"I never did whip them or nothing, spank them," she says. "I used to talk to them."

Adds Vera, "And she would ground us. Like if you didn't go to church, or you played sick, then you couldn't go to the movie theater. Forget that—you wasn't going.

"Where we used to live on Derbigny Street, there was a ball park, where the guys would play ball games at night against another team. And like if I wanted to go sit outside and watch them, 'No, get in here! Come inside! Don't be out there looking at them men. Come inside!' "

Vera, Mildred and I have a good laugh at Mildred's old-fashioned ways as Vera continues.

"And look—I had a boyfriend I was trying to sneak one time. She told June take me to the movies. And so me and him went to the movies—the Gallo show. And the boy met us there. The boy was sitting next to me: This the boy, this me, this June. So as me and the boy were just talking, June would say, 'Buy me some popcorn.' And then I said O.K. I let him go get the popcorn, because I had my allowance. He come back, 'Buy me a cold drink,' and I give him money to get the cold drink. And he come back, 'I want a Long Boy candy.' I say I don't have no more money. 'I'm gonna tell momma.'

"I got so tired of that. I said, 'You know what you do, June? Tell her. Tell her.' I was like twenty years old. I said, 'Go ahead and tell her.' "

Says Mildred, "My momma was strict, too. She never had no problem with her children. My brothers and sisters, they was number one. She never had no problem with them. They never went to jail, never go stealing, never did nothing like that, no indeed. She raised them like that. And I was just like her."

She shares her hopes for her children and grandchildren. "I would like for them to be good, and do the right thing, like I was," Mildred says. "They'll never be like me. No indeed. Too much old."

Vera points out that times are different for young people now. There are more distractions, more dangers, and so many things in which to be involved.

"Time moving," says Vera.

***

When Mildred and Vic moved to Louisiana Avenue Parkway they were the first black family on the street. Then another black family moved in next door and for a while there were just two black families between South Claiborne Avenue and South Broad Avenue. Mildred and Vic met no hostility here.

"The white people, they was nice to us," says Mildred. "Because my husband didn't associate. My husband was a kind of careful person about associating. So he always was sitting in the back. And they was all rich, millionaire people, around here."

The Victorians fit in with their esteemed neighbors. Vera used to babysit Mayor LaToya Cantrell's child and still considers Mayor Cantrell a friend. Former New Orleans first lady Verna Satterlee, wife of Moon Landrieu and mother of former Mayor Mitch Landrieu, has visited Mildred at home. She was accompanied by a man who stayed outside.

"He's just a walking, up and down," Mildred recalls. "And I asked her, 'Who is that man walking in the front like that?' And she say, 'Oh, that's the policeman that walked me here, to watch for me. I told him I was coming by your house.' And all he was doing is walking in front. And everybody was looking at him.

"She sat on my porch a long time," Mildred remembers.

Not one for the clubs, she has seen June play a few times.

"Time back, yeah," she says. But she'd "rather be home. Vera used to go. My husband, too."

She is proud that June graduated from Werlein's on Canal Street, Houston's School of Music on Claiborne, and Xavier University.

"He graduated three times," she says.

She listens with lively interest, laughing occasionally as Vera shares a funny story about June and Dog, from when they were playing together in Kenner.

Says Vera, "They would always give me the car. They would never give it to him. And I was driving him and Preston, the one beat the drums. And he comes to me and tells me he going to the car to get his guitar strings. And some kind of way he start the car and pulled off—

and went in the bar. In the bar! The car was in the bar. All the bricks was on top of the car. Do you remember that, momma?"

Mildred indicates that she does indeed remember.

"And that's when daddy had surgery on his eye," Vera continues. "And when I called and told daddy, and I was crying, daddy made Charles bring him out there. And the people kept saying, 'Call the police, call the police!' And that man said, 'I'm not calling no police.' He said, 'This my place.' And then he said, 'Let me run my place.' And they didn't have no children, and he loveded June, that man—'Son.' They used to call him Son. And my daddy said, 'Well I'll pay for the damage he do.' And he said, 'No no no,' he said, 'It's all right.' And that's what he did."

[June remembers that night so well. He was sitting with Dog in the car. If the truth were told, they were a little bit high. They were on top of the world, really, a couple of guys who with their band mates could turn a dismal backstreet saloon into a jumping showplace, packing it with friends and music fans, and drinkers, bringing "the girls"—enthusiastic dancers. It might have been June's best times. They were making a lot of money for Son. He would have given the bar to June at some point, if June ever wanted to sit still and run it, which he did not. Outside Son's that night, June and Dog felt high and carefree, and got careless. One of them suggested they "get up" out of there. In the driver's seat and confused, June started the Chevrolet and searched for the right gear. He chose "R" for "right" and hit the gas, reversing into the club.]

According to Vera nobody was hurt. "Everybody broke out and ran," she says as her mother enjoys a long laugh. "I ran, too, and I didn't know why I was running. I ran, and I didn't know what was going on. Then when we get outside they say, 'Somebody done ran the car in the place!' And when I looked it was the car—momma car—I almost died! I was crying so much!

"He got me in trouble because they give me the keys, and I always would drive him. And he asked me for the keys to go get guitar strings. I don't know what he was doing. 'Why you start it up?' I say. 'The guitar strings in the trunk!' "

Hurricane Katrina

"When the high water came through here, I went to my brother's in Baton Rouge," Mildred says. "He had his own house and everything. He say, 'Y'all come here.' He say, 'I'm going to be waiting for y'all.' He was waiting right there in the street, waiting for us. And we stayed to him, long as we couldn't come back here. And he didn't want me to come back. He said, 'Stay here, don't go back, you don't know what's going to happen again.' I said, 'No, I've got to go back and see about my house.' Then I came back. And way after that, he died. He was like ninety-six when he died.

"I'll be ninety-five next birthday, in August," says Mildred.

On August 28, 2005, there was supposed to be a belated party celebrating her eightieth birthday but instead she and Vera evacuated on the orders of Mayor Ray Nagin.

"I had my cake and everything, we had to take my cake to my brother's," Mildred says.

Says Vera, "On the twenty-eighth I was making a big pot of gumbo. We was having a get-together. But we had to leave when the mayor said it was mandatory—that everybody get out of here. Which people didn't. A lot of people stayed. But I told momma it's time to go. So we left. I left my brand-new van. I had just finished paying for it about four months."

Says Mildred, "It drowned, yeah, it drowned." Also the family Lincoln.

She and Vera don't overstate their losses. Nearly two thousand people died here in Louisiana and elsewhere on the Gulf Coast.

It was a trying ordeal for them, nonetheless. They returned to months of work needing to be done on the house, and everything in Mildred's house lost. Vera, being upstairs, did not flood but had to live without water or electricity or neighbors. Mildred stayed with her first cousin, Nita, her father's sister's daughter, now deceased.

As Vera tells it, "When we were allowed to come back, we were living on Saratoga and Napoleon, by my aunt's. So I started coming here, and I would sleep upstairs by myself, and leave momma by Napoleon. And it was so funny because the National Guard, I don't care when I would come back here at night time, I don't know if it was some kind of satellite or something. And it was only two families, back here, Broad to Claiborne. Me, and not the house next door, but the next one. And the National Guard would pull up. And they shined the lights on me and they would get out with their guns in their hands and they would ask me, 'Where do you live?' And I would tell them I live right here. And they would ask me, 'What's your address?' And I would tell them. I told them I come and stay here, because the people coming every morning at six o'clock, to work on the house. So they say, 'O.K. come on, we're going to walk you to the door.' And they would come to the door and I would put my key in and they would let me in, and they say, 'We're going to watch out for you.' And I say, 'Thank you very much.' That's why, a lot of people was against the National Guard, but me, I praise them.

Because if it wasn't for them I could have been dead, killed, you know? If anybody knew I was here by myself.

"And I would go upstairs and get in the bed with no light, no water, nothing, nothing going on. And I could just say my prayers. And at night I would see the light from their cars passing, turning. I'd say, 'That's the National Guard passing there, watching over me: the Lord, and them, watching over me.' "

Lillian

In my world
You got to take your chances
If you want to be free.
Ain't nothing guaranteed, oh no.
Take your chances.

- June Victory and the Bayou Renegades, 'Take Your Chances'

It is hard to separate the musician from the criminal in June, hard to say where the mudjacking stopped and the gambling began, hard to say how many jails and prisons June has been in and for which crimes. His jobs and run-ins have overlapped, been entwined, one dependent on the other sometimes. He has been a longshoreman and a street lawyer. He has been both predator, and prey.

And so it is with the females in his life—the four women with whom he has had or has raised children. He wants them recognized in his book, but separated in a way that is hard to do.

A woman might be excused for throwing her man out if he came home early one morning from work with a guitar case full of acid. Lillian helped June however she could, and was there for him while he worked all night for Sol Owens, and cheering for him up against the stage at G.T.O. and Sabou.

If a man came home early in the morning tripping and determined to carry out a vendetta against his brother-in-law there is no telling what his girlfriend might do. When June came home early in the morning rearing to go after his brother-in-law, Lillian, despite being pregnant, went uptown with him.

June remembers Lillian as tough and loyal, attributes June also has and the ones he is most proud of in himself.

Cheryl

At Cabbage Alley and the Parisian, Cheryl cheered her man June Victory, the life of the party, the guitar player and renegade Indian. Cheryl never gave up on June; but there are some hard feelings and children involved and June wants peace for the children, and their mother. Sometimes the less said, the better, but June will never forget Cheryl.

'Ping-Ponging'

"Cheryl was from Uptown, so automatically, they didn't associate with the Downtown girls," June says. "So I got a Downtown girl, Lillian, and Cheryl was Uptown. Cheryl was going to the Parisian Room, and Cabbage Alley. So I wouldn't let Lillian come to the Parisian Room. Lillian could have went to two clubs: the G.T.O. and Sabou. So they both had two different locations. So I went on a while with that. I would live with Lillian maybe a month, live with Cheryl a month, Ping-Ponging, 'cause I didn't want to just keep one of them. Because the kids was gonna grow up and say, 'Well, you turned your back on us.' So Lillian say, 'What you gonna do?' I say, 'I'm going to leave both of you guys. I won't live with you. I'll be living with Cheryl sometimes.' And so Lillian was cool, she agreed to that.

"I was doing that for a long time, and I say, you know what, I'm going to just start a new life. So I quit the music business, and I went out and found a wife, that I wanted to marry."

Jackie

"So I found Jacquelyn—Victory because she married me. She was from the Ninth Ward. She had a house on Tonti Street, not far from Desire Street, back up in that area. After a while talking to her I moved in with her. And I went into the construction business. I didn't tell her I played music. But she would come to me and say, 'June, such-and-such a person say you a guitar player,' and I say, 'No.' "

They were married in June's house in Metairie, by a preacher. "It was a house wedding. It was almost by the spillway," he says.

"At that particular time, I parked Cheryl, I parked Lillian. I didn't want her to know none of these people. I changed my life, got a wife, started a new life, opened up a construction company. I kept the construction company all the way up to the gambling operation. Me and Jackie still together. We had it working. She was running a bingo hall on Airline Highway and we got in trouble. 'Cause it was a nonprofit thing. The feds came in and said the employee say—one of the volunteer workers say we was paying 'em—so by her being young, I hurry up and put her in the military, so she wouldn't be able to face charges. The other people, they wound up getting in trouble, so they had to shut it down.

"So she went in the military. We's still married. But she found out I was a musician. ... Her girlfriend called and found my car by Cheryl's house. Cheryl never gave up.

"So I stayed with Jackie a while and I left and went overseas, and when I got back, I didn't go back to Jackie. I went home, to my house, by my mom's, and I locked myself up because I was under house arrest. I locked up, and I couldn't come off of the map. Jackie would come 'round to see me. And she said well the military told her that she had to divorce me, because it was a high risk for her career. Because she was working in cyanide and stuff, and that's kind of dangerous, you know, because it make bullets. So she came for a divorce, so I say O.K. Then she come back—she didn't want the divorce. So she was confused. 'What I'm gonna do? Divorce him? Stay with him?' So we broke up."

Ivory

"When I met Ivory I was with Tina, a girlfriend, you know, just out the blue. And that's when my little cousin named Verdell introduced me to Ivory, said Ivory needed help.

"Ivory was disabled, and she was trying to get her Social Security benefits, and (her attorney) for seven years wasn't getting nowhere. So I had attorney skill, I knew the law. I worked under Ellis Pailet and Mary Ann McGrath Swaim. I was at my mom's house and I looked at her paperwork, and I found errors. It was so much work, I moved with Verdell—she was the next door apartment, to Ivory. So there was so much going on I moved into Ivory's house, in the Iberville Projects. And I started the paperwork. And it was a lot. And it was hard.

"Not only she was trying to get money from Social Security, she also was injured in a chemical accident, what led to the train litigation. A boxcar leaked, where she was living at somewhere, and it was a special master case. So I'm working with that and I'm working with this thing. At the same time I take off on the road because I started recording music. And Ivory went with me on the road and they made her president of the paraphernalia company, because Frank Quintini likeded Ivory, trusted her.

"And we stayed in the project. But it was so much

chaos in that project. It was one of the worst places you could live in. Everybody knew Ivory because Ivory would walk around selling pies, they called her the Pie Lady, and she would sell pies. She also had a sweet shop in her house. She would sell nachos, ice cream, anything to make a quarter, a nickel and a dime, to survive.

"So we're going on and on. It was bad in that project. That project was like, crazy. For one thing, I went in there and I wasn't supposed to go in the Iberville. I'm from Uptown. And that was a challenge for me, to get in there and take over my spot. My attorney, my mom, my dad, everybody was worried, said 'Man, it's too dangerous,' but I got in there and made my point, so everything was cool, you know, I made it. All you have to do is be a stand-up guy, and handle your business. I made it with the guys up in there. But they was very corrupted and stuff. A lot of murders was going on, it was unreal.

"The police was watching me, because I had a lot of white guys with me. I set up a recording studio in the project.

"I was working on a re-injury case for Ivory. She was injured in a car accident. I represented her in court, and won. And that was good. The same day I went in for trial, I won. I went under decree, and I worked for the judge, and the judge awarded Ivory.

"I was handling her litigation case for the train litigation and I got her ten thousand, for that case, and a few thousand for this other thing. She had a serious nerve problem. She already had chronic pains. She went to mental health, you know, because her way of thinking, all that played a part of it. But she got awarded ten thousand and her baby daughter, I got her money. And then they came back and paid off again.

"Then I went into another case, Social Security started paying her, and I got the third case that went up to two hundred something thousand, that was good. ...

"When Katrina hit, we was in the Iberville Project that day. And all of a sudden the water started rising. So, I didn't want to leave New Orleans. Well, I was in denial. I was running from one place to another in the water. And that's when Ivory, she say, 'June, we're going to have to get out.' So I say O.K. I found a place, some people was running a camp not far from Poydras Street, where they got boats. So I went and talked to them. And they took me to the airport.

"When I got to the airport, Armstrong Airport, it was so many people, man, it was like crazy. So I was trying to figure out where they was going, where they was taking people. So they came back talking about Houston, Texas. I say, 'No, we not going to Houston. Let me get outta here.' 'What you gonna do?' I say, 'Hold up.' I got on a bus that was going to Shreveport-Bossier City. So that's where I went. I got there, I couldn't get nothing going. We was living in a hockey arena. They set it up. And I stayed there. And she met Diane and those people, and they wanted me to go there. I said no. I went in the 'hood, you know me, I went in the 'hood where I can operate, so they was nervous about me in the 'hood in Shreveport. But I met a preacher, and he likeded me, and he hooked me up with a nice place.

"We came back to New Orleans, the storm was dried out, and found her brother. We found him, and left for Minnesota. While I was in Minnesota I got with Marc Morial. He was president of the Urban League. I met a lady at this place where they was doing applications, her name was Ms. Williams, she heard about me from New Orleans—from booking the band. So she was retiring, she said I'm not going to retire: I'm going to get you back on your feet. So she got me a house. I wound up with three houses. I said d- what I'm gonna do? So I gave Ivory a house; I took two. She gave me a voucher to go get brand-new furniture. Here I go again! So I put all the furniture in my house. And Ivory was getting a lot of help in her place, so she didn't want to stay there, she moved in me house, so she wound up with all the furniture and everything.

"Frank Quintini came. So what I was doing in Minnesota is doing gigs. I mostly would go out like I do in New Orleans now and sit in, get the feel of people, and do like that. But I wasn't making any money. And I already had been to Minnesota in the past—when I was working at Tracy Chapman's, with Bo Dollis and Prince and all of them. So that was way beyond this. But when I got back to Minnesota people knew me. I was performing at the Viking club. I was getting paid for that gig. It was a good job: short hours, working on tips, making good money, playing mostly my stuff—and some blues.

"When I left New Orleans, remember, the case was still pending, for the re-injury case, I was doing for Ivory. I hadn't got that money yet. But all of a sudden it happened, and they was ready to pay off. By the time Ivory got through living off a lot of the money, I found out they had sixty-six thousand left, so I took that and made it work. And that was it.

"We came back to New Orleans and we living right now on Tchoupitoulas. That's where the dog park, and you, come in. It's over."

Ivory's Okra Gumbo

- Two cartons beef broth—poured in the pot.
- Two boxes Zatarain's Shrimp Creole mixed in a half-pitcher of hot water poured into the pot.
- Let it come to a boil.
- Add a box of crab boil "to give the gumbo a taste."
- Add one pack of chicken wings cut at the joints.
- Add half a bag of smoked sausage, sliced "not too thin but kind of thin."
- Add the "season"—chopped onion, bell pepper, celery, green onions.
- Add salt and pepper.
- Wait to cook real good, then add two pounds of shrimp.
- Boil into a gravy "not too thick, water-thick" thirty to forty minutes then add eight washed, cleaned, broken-in-half crabs, and okra cooked separately in grease until all the slime is out.
- Takes about an hour and a half to make—feeds fifteen to twenty people or more—serve more juicy than meaty to "stretch further."

And some final advice from the cook:

"You got to taste it yourself. If it tastes good to you, it'll taste good to anybody."##

Notes

June Victory was interviewed from 2016 through 2019, mostly in my car on the streets of New Orleans and surrounds; but also at my house on Tchoupitoulas Street; in June's living room, also on Tchoupitoulas Street; on the road from New Roads to New Orleans; between shows; at Wisner Park dog-run; at the Bay St. Louis, Mississippi, beach, where we went on a lark; and via correspondence, with recordings via iPhone, i.e. Geek device, and an old-school cassette recorder. I have notes in a reporter's notebook, on stationery from two hotels, on sticky notes and a dinner napkin.

Vera Sterling was interviewed from 2017 through 2019, in person and via telephone, and was always helpful with information and stories. Given half a chance she will produce two photo albums stuffed with memorabilia about Indians and June, Indians and June. She is so proud of the New Orleans Indians, of her brother, her family and her city. She can also tell you exactly what is wrong with any one or all of them, and how to fix it.

Big Chief Little Walter Cook welcomed me into the Creole Wild West family as he took to the streets on Mardi Gras Day 2018 and 2019; unforgettable, colorful, rich affairs. I was star-struck when I saw 'dem Indians running. Walter's touch is all over New Orleans in some of the prettiest Indian suits. In beads and stitches, and dyes of all colors, he is leaving his mark on history. I'm glad I was there to see it.

Mark Appleford was interviewed in April 2018 at Funky 544, Bourbon Street.

Lefty Keith was interviewed in April 2018 at Funky 544, Bourbon Street.

Mike Christopher was interviewed in September 2019 via telephone.

Chief Kenny Young was interviewed in September 2019 via telephone.

Ernie Vincent was interviewed in September 2019 via telephone.

Earl Johnson was interviewed in September 2019 via telephone.

Mildred Victorian was interviewed in October 2019 at her residence.

Earl Nunez and Jasmin Cardriche were interviewed in October and November 2019 as we rushed around for rehearsal and a show. Earl answered questions by follow-up telephone interview.

Google was a good source for leads on information about Mardi Gras Indians. YouTube is a good place to get an introduction to the Indian songs and some of the gangs/tribes.

Wikipedia is a frequent source of information for me and has interesting articles about Mardi Gras Indians, including biographies of several of the Big Chiefs mentioned in this book.

The Times Picayune and NOLA.com, and *The New Orleans Advocate* were constant sources of information about New Orleans while I did my research. Also helpful were the reporting of *OffBeat Magazine* and *The Louisiana Weekly,* and the Uptown Messenger. The Messenger's story on Central City becoming a "food desert" cited in

the chapter "The Return of Cabbage Alley" can be found here:
http://uptownmessenger.com/2019/09/dryades-public-market-closure-leaves-a-food-desert-in-central-city/

Quoted extensively were lyrics gleaned from the music CD *June Victory and the Bayou Renegades*, 1998, Monkey Hill Records, New Orleans; songs by June Victory, published by Wilson Victory Publishing, B.M.I.; lyrics used by permission and in cooperation with the songwriter/publisher. Other credits not mentioned in the text: engineered by Jack Berry; mastered by Parker Dinkins. I listened to it over and over, from the Indian shout kicking off "Down on the Bayou" to the last notes of "The Real Deal." It represents thousands of years of music making: I hear echoes of stick-and-turtle-shell instruments and also of country and disco but its strongest flavor is just good old rock 'n' roll. They call it 'Indian funk.' I can't wait to hear more.

The website Carnival New Orleans News, at news.carnivalneworleans.com, has a comprehensive article by NewOrleansMusicMan covering the many twists and turns of June Victory's music career, his entry into the mudjacking business, his relationship with Frank Quintini and their adventures in Minnesota after Hurricane Katrina, and other business enterprises and escapades. The Website puts June among such Mardi Gras legends as Al "Carnival Time" Johnson, Blain Kern's Mardi Gras World, and the Mardi Gras krewes. Headlined "Mardi Gras Music Series - June Victory & The Bayou Renegades" (http://blog.carnivalneworleans.com/?p=2503), the article captures a complicated picture and adds to June's story with photos, a biography, and media reviews of

June's work. Several Bayou Renegades songs are also embedded in the article. "Somebody, whoever they are, had to of been following this for a long time, to write this kind of stuff that's in this phone, yeah," June says. "That kill it," he says of the site. "That cover everything that you said in that book. It's worser than that, 'cause it tell about armed robbery and this and that. So, that's what's so good about it. Because they already exploited this. You say if they want to know more, go to this Website, and that's when they're going to get caught up. When they go to New Orleans Carnival time, and they go to reading it, they're going to find out how f-'d up this thing is. That's a lot of stuff in that phone." The website also has a lot of information about some of the other Indians mentioned in this book. Of particular interest to me was the article headlined "Bo Dollis & the Wild Magnolias" (http://blog.carnivalneworleans.com/?p=2970). June's favorite review reprinted on the Carnival New Orleans News site is by Geraldine Wyckoff: "The music here is best described as 'the Meters meets the Mardi Gras Indians,' " writes Wyckoff.

For additional reading on the Mardi Gras Indians, especially on the role of the Big Chief in the community and the work of the New Orleans Mardi Gras Indian Council, I recommend Al Kennedy's excellent book *Chief of Chiefs: Robert Nathaniel Lee and the Mardi Gras Indians of New Orleans, 1915-2001* (Gretna Publishing Co., 2018).

I want to thank those who read early chapters or drafts of this book, for their time and input: my dad William Franklin Andrews and mother Carolyn; my wife Ginny Andrews; Vera Sterling; Schelita White; Carla Chamberlain; Margaret Marley Armstrong; Monica Clark; Ernie Vincent; Chief Kenny Young; Earl Johnson;

Mike Christopher; and Geraldine Wyckoff.

Additional thanks are surely due to my dad, my brother Victor, and Toni at the appraisal office in Tennessee, who all carried a portion of my workload while I lived the dream down in New Orleans.

And a final note to readers: If you spot an error in this book, please help correct it for future editions. Contact brentandrews1973@yahoo.com.

-Brent Andrews
Hermitage, Tennessee, January 22, 2020

About the Author

A former editor of the Middle Tennessee State University student newspaper *Sidelines*, Thomas Brent Andrews covered government and crime as a reporter for newspapers in Tennessee and Idaho between 1995 and 2001, when he joined the family real estate appraisal business in Franklin, Tennessee. He has published six books since 2005, including his self-help book for alcoholics, *The Pot Plan*. He and the former Ginny Stallard have been married since 1994 and have two children, Price Stallard and Violet Stallard Andrews. Brent, Ginny and Violet lived in New Orleans from 2015 to 2018 while Violet attended Lusher Charter School. Price is married and teaches high school physics in Murfreesboro, Tennessee.

More Chronic Discontent Books

The Pot Plan: Louie B. Stumblin and the War on Drugs by Thomas Brent Andrews

From Humble Beginnings: Songs of a Native Son by William Franklin Andrews

The Greatest Revolution by Jim Sullivan

Prison is a Place by Harley Sorensen

From Humble Beginnings: Tales of a Native Son by William Franklin Andrews

Coming Soon

Uptown with Freddie and Meaux by Thomas Brent Andrews

Minnesota Man by Harley Sorensen

On the Web

http://chronicdiscontent.blogspot.com

Made in the USA
Columbia, SC
27 April 2022